HOUGHTON MIFFLIN HARCOURT

WRITE SOURCE

TEACHER'S EDITION

Grade 2

Authors
Dave Kemper, Patrick Sebranek, and Verne Meyer

Illustrator
Chris Krenzke

GREAT
SOURCE.

 HOUGHTON MIFFLIN HARCOURT

Reviewers

Genevieve Bodnar NBCT
Youngstown City Schools
Youngstown, Ohio

Mary M. Fischer
Arlington Public Schools
Arlington, Massachusetts

Cynthia Fontenot
Green T. Lindon Elementary
Lafayette, Louisiana

Heather Hagstrum
Unified School District #475
Ft. Riley, Kansas

Lisa Kickbusch
Pattonville School District
St. Ann, Missouri

Michele A. Lewis
Pattonville School District
St. Ann, Missouri

Joyce Martin
Forest Ridge Elementary
  School
Howard County
Laurel, Maryland

Kim T. Mickle
Alief Independent School
  District
Houston, Texas

Lisa D. Miller
Greater Clark County Schools
Jeffersonville, Indiana

Karen A. Reid
Rosemead School District
Rosemead, California

Roslyn Rowley-Penk
Renton School District
Renton, Washington

Jeannine M. Shirley, M. Ed.
White Hall School District
White Hall, Arkansas

Tanya Smith
Frankford Elementary School
Frankford, Delaware

WRITE SOURCE Online
www.hmheducation.com/writesource

Photos: TE-8 ©Tim Pannell/Corbis; TE-10–TE-11 ©Andrzej Tokarski/Alamy; TE-12 ©Image Source/Getty Images; TE-16–TE-17 Harcourt.

Text: Common Core State Standards © Copyright 2010. National Governors Association Center for Best Practices and Council of Chief State School Officers. All rights reserved.

Printed in the U.S.A.

ISBN   978-0-547-48434-1

1 2 3 4 5 6 7 8 9 10   0914   19 18 17 16 15 14 13 12 11 10

4500000000   A B C D E F G

Program Overview

Professional Development for Writing

THE FORMS, THE PROCESS, AND THE TRAITS

WRITING WORKSHOP AND GRAMMAR

WRITING ACROSS THE CURRICULUM, ACADEMIC VOCABULARY, AND TEST PREPARATION

DIFFERENTIATION

RESEARCH

Teacher Resources

In the Front Matter

In the Wraparound

The Writing Process

The Forms of Writing

How does *Write Source* work?

Write Source is a complete language arts curriculum focused on writing and grammar in print and digital formats.

With writing instruction at the core, grammar, usage, and mechanics are taught in an authentic writing context.

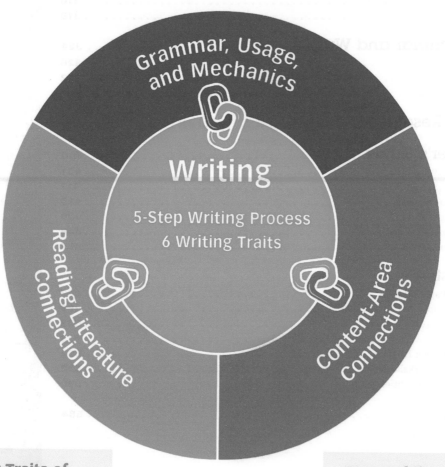

Grammar, Usage, and Mechanics

Reading/Literature Connections

Content-Area Connections

Writing
5-Step Writing Process
6 Writing Traits

The Six Traits of Effective Writing
- Ideas
- Organization
- Voice
- Word Choice
- Sentence Fluency
- Conventions

Steps of the Writing Process
- Prewriting
- Writing
- Revising
- Editing
- Publishing

Introduce the writing form:

- Read authentic real-world fiction or nonfiction that models the writing form.
- Analyze a model paragraph.
- Preview the form by responding to questions about the model and by writing a paragraph.

Each core forms of writing unit follows the same instructional path—a consistent writing curriculum across all grade levels.

Explore the writing form:

- Analyze a model story or essay.
- Read authentic real-world fiction or nonfiction that models the writing form.
- Use the writing process to write a story or essay.
- Use the six traits to revise and then edit the writing for conventions.

Write in the content areas:

- Write a piece in the same writing form across the major content areas—science, social studies, math, and the arts.

Write for assessment:

- Using the unit's writing form, write a piece for assessment.

Write Source prepares students for success in the 21st century.

What are the main components of *Write Source?*

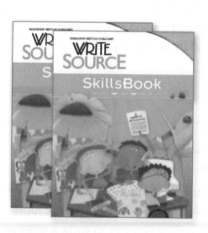

The **Assessment** book provides a pretest, progress tests, and a post-test.

The **Daily Language Workouts** build student conventions skills through quick, daily editing and proofreading activities.

The *Write Source* **Student Edition** reflects the latest research on writing instruction. The **Teacher's Edition** has all the support you need to help students become confident, proficient writers.

The **SkillsBook** helps students practice and improve grammar, usage, and mechanics skills.

Write Source Online
www.hmheducation.com/writesource

- **Interactive Whiteboard Lessons** build background and promote interest in writing.

- The **Net-text** provides an interactive alternative to core print instruction.

- **GrammarSnap** brings multimedia fun to key grammar topics.

- The **Online Portfolio** gives students a place to share their best work.

- The searchable **File Cabinet** offers a number of resources for differentiating and supplementing instruction.

How does the Teacher's Edition support instruction?

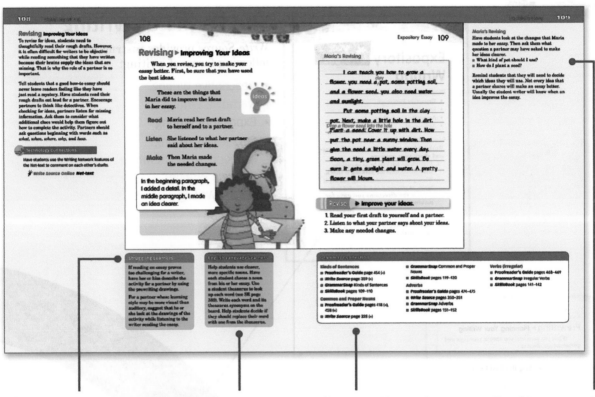

Differentiated Instruction for struggling learners and advanced learners is provided throughout the core instructional units.

The Teacher's Edition provides consistent support for **English language learners.**

Grammar Connections support grammar, usage, and mechanics instruction.

Teaching suggestions and activity answers provide the support you need to implement writing instruction.

Additional Resources

- Common Core State Standards Correlation
- Yearlong Timetable
- Professional Development for Writing

- Reading–Writing Connection
- "Getting Started" Copy Masters
- Benchmark Papers
- Graphic Organizers
- Family Letters

How is *Write Source* organized?

The Forms of Writing

Write Source provides instruction in the following forms of writing:

- Descriptive Writing
- Narrative Writing
- Expository Writing
- Persuasive Writing
- Responding to Literature
- Creative Writing
- Report Writing

The Writing Process

This unit introduces students to the steps in the writing process and integrates instruction on the six traits of writing.

The Tools of Learning

This third section helps students improve important classroom skills: giving speeches, writing in journals and learning logs, viewing and listening, and taking tests.

Basic Grammar and Writing

This section covers the fundamental building blocks of writing: words, sentences, and paragraphs.

A Writer's Resource

This section is a writing guide students can refer to whenever they have questions about the development and presentation of paragraphs, reports, essays, and stories.

Proofreader's Guide

The final section addresses the conventions of standard English: punctuation, mechanics, spelling, grammar, usage, and sentences.

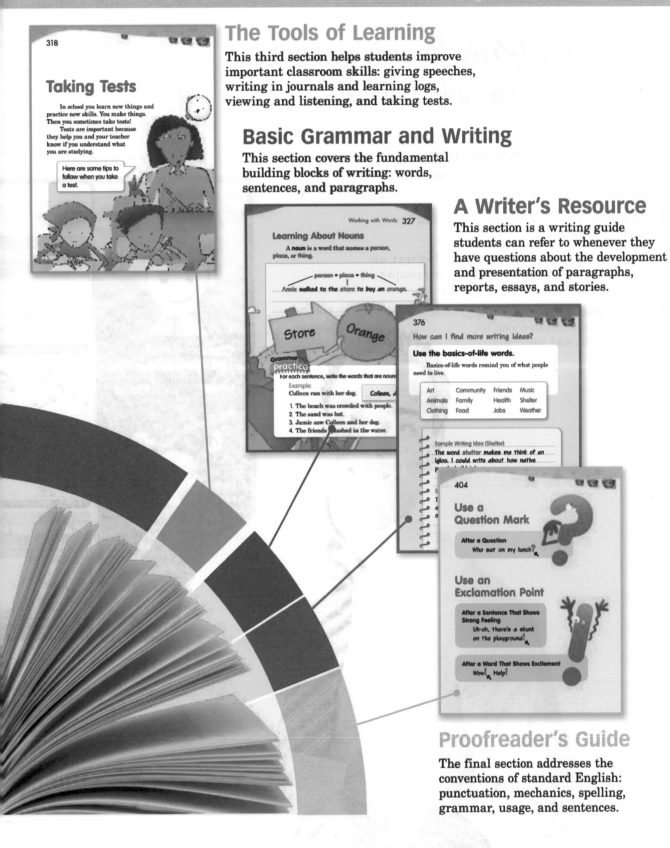

How does *Write Source* support today's digital-age learners?

*W*rite Source Online taps into the power of interactivity and motivation to deliver a coordinated, comprehensive technology program that empowers teachers to . . .

- build an early foundation in writing and key grammar skills

- deliver **interactive instruction** using Net-text, an easy-to-use online application featuring complete writing support

- engage students in the writing process through **customizable avatars, dashboards, and electronic portfolios**

Teacher Dashboard

Mr. Rodriguez

WRITE So

Narrative Wri

Class:
Third Period English

Change   Sign out

Punctuation R

FFLIN HARCOURT

Write Source Online
www.hmheducation.com/writesource

Preparing students and teachers for success in the 21st century.

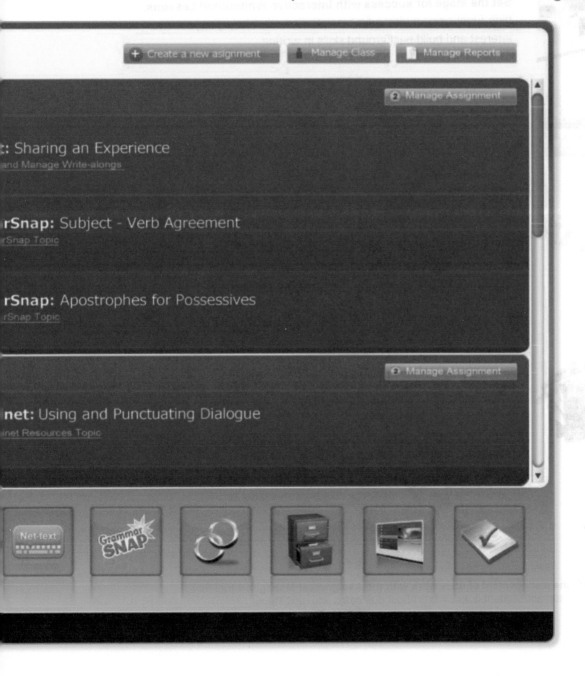

What are the components of *Write Source Online?*

Set the stage for success with Interactive Whiteboard Lessons, high-functioning multimedia presentations that help you promote interest and build background skills in writing.

Transform students into aspiring young writers with Net-text, an online application that features full audio, click-and-reveal instruction, useful checklists, and more.

Put the fun into grammar with GrammarSnap, a multimedia application that builds foundation in key topics through videos, games, and quizzes.

Students can use SkillSnap points earned in GrammarSnap to unlock a variety of accessories for their personal avatar.

Tap into the power of publishing with the *Write Source Online* Portfolio, a customizable resource that gives students an authentic forum for sharing their writing.

With teacher support, students can connect with each other in My Network to share their published pieces.

Simplify the management of daily work with the Assignment Manager, a tool that delivers automatic student notifications about due dates and next steps.

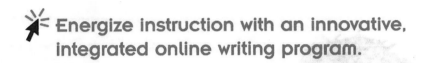

Energize instruction with an innovative, integrated online writing program.

instructional videos

plays
literature connections
graphic organizers
satire
presentation   creative writing   online peer reviewing
compare

process
poetry   grammar   writing   writing in the arts   word ch
descriptive writing   collaboration   voice   mechanics
prewriting   paragraph   expository writing   assessment
stories   rubric   publishing
Write Source Online
www.hmheducation.com/writesource
traits   editing
ideas
writing across the curriculum   interactive instrucion
essay scoring   revising   narrative writing   essay   organization
sentence fluency   conventions   usage
informative   writing forms   games
benchmark papers   writing in math   persuasive writing   npt

Additional Resources

- **Bookshelf** *Write Source* print component eBooks
- **File Cabinet** Additional resources, such as blackline masters and additional assessments, that help you minimize planning time and differentiate instruction

Professional Development for Writing

This section of the *Write Source* Teacher's Edition provides information to help you make the most of *Write Source* in your classroom. The program's instructional design includes comprehensive support for the topics that matter most to teachers: grammar, writing workshops, academic vocabulary, test preparation, the use of technology, and so much more. Whether you are a new teacher or a veteran, the information in the following pages will show how *Write Source* can help you meet your classroom goals.

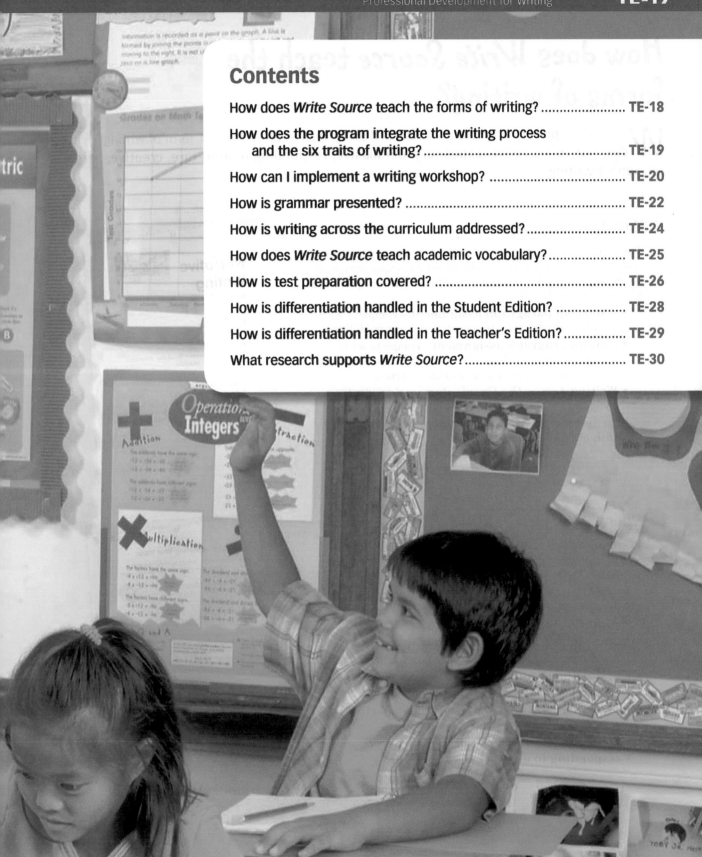

Contents

How does *Write Source* teach the forms of writing?

Write Source provides numerous models and assignments for each major form of writing: **descriptive, narrative, expository, persuasive, responding to literature, creative,** and **report writing**.

Writing Assignments

The core writing units provide students with comprehensive, research-based exploration of the narrative, expository, and persuasive forms of writing. Each of these units employs the following instructional sequence:

- a **start-up paragraph assignment**—complete with a writing model and step-by-step writing guidelines
- a **multiparagraph assignment**—complete with writing models, in-depth step-by-step guidelines, and integration of traits and grammar instruction
- **Writing Across the Curriculum assignments**—complete with writing models and writing tips
- an **assessment writing assignment**—complete with a model response to a prompt plus writing tips

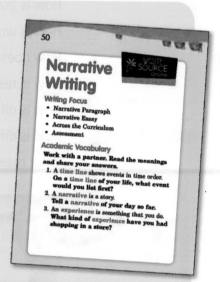

Writing Skills and Strategies

As students develop their compositions in each unit, they use the following skills and strategies in a wide variety of contexts:

- reading and responding to texts (writing models)
- **integrating the traits of writing into the writing process**
- using graphic organizers
- developing beginnings, middles, and endings
- **practicing grammar skills in context**
- publishing (presenting) writing
- **assessing with an analytical, mode-specific scoring rubric**
- reflecting on writing
- **responding to an assessment prompt**

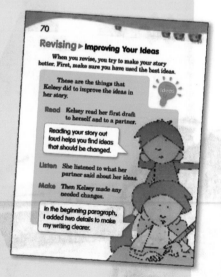

How does the program integrate the writing process and the traits?

Throughout each core forms of writing unit, the six traits of effective writing are integrated into the steps of the writing process. As students develop their writing, they acquire an understanding of and appreciation for each trait of writing. In addition, a rubric, checklists, guidelines, and activities are used to ensure that each piece of writing is completely traits based.

The Process and the Traits in the Core Units

Goals for Writing
This page helps students understand the goals of their writing. It lists expectations for each trait as it relates to the writing form.

Revising and Editing for the Traits
When students are ready to revise and edit, they will find guidelines and strategies to help them improve their writing for each of the featured traits.

Rubrics for the Core Units
A traits-based rubric concludes each unit. This rubric ties directly to the goal chart at the beginning of the unit and to revising and editing pages.

Special Note: For more information about the writing traits, we recommend *Creating Writers Through 6-Trait Writing Assessment and Instruction*, 4th ed., by Vicki Spandel (Addison Wesley Longman, 2005) and *Write Traits®* by Vicki Spandel and Jeff Hicks (Houghton Mifflin Harcourt, 2011).

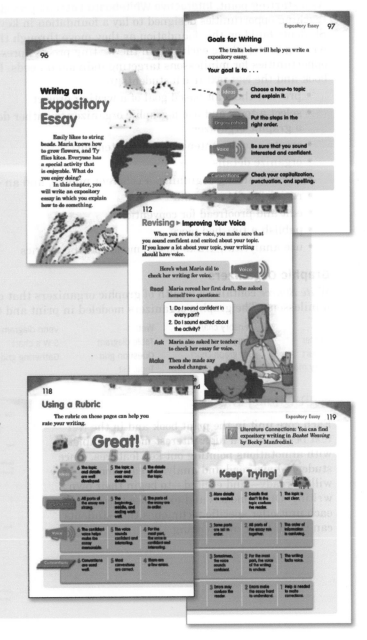

How can I implement a writing workshop?

*W*rite Source supports a workshop approach through both print and technology resources. The program includes minilessons for instruction, high-quality models to encourage writing, support for whole-class sharing, and much more.

Integrated Minilessons

As a starting point, **Interactive Whiteboard Lessons** provide short, focused teaching opportunities designed to lay a foundation in key concepts. Students build on this foundation as they move through the core forms of writing units, where each step in the writing process presents additional opportunities for minilessons targeting individual needs. Both the print book and the **Net-text** teach students to:

- preview the trait-based goal of a writing project
- select a topic and use a graphic organizer to gather details using a graphic organizer
- create a topic sentence (thesis statement)
- organize details
- create a strong beginning, a coherent middle, and an effective ending
- revise for the six traits
- edit and proofread for conventions
- publish a finished piece
- use analytical, (traits-based) mode-specific rubrics

Mon	Tues	Wed	Thurs	Fri
Writing Minilessons (10 minutes as needed)				
Status Checks (2 minutes) Find out what students will work on for the day.				
Individual Work (30 minutes) Writing, Revising, Editing, Conferencing, or Publishing				
Whole-Class Sharing Session (5 minutes)				

Graphic Organizers

Write Source contains a wealth of graphic organizers that can serve as the subject of minilessons. The graphic organizers modeled in print and technology include the following:

List	Sensory chart	Web	Venn diagram	Basics-of-life list
Cluster	Storyboard	Table diagram	5 W's chart	Picture diagram
T-chart	Bar graph chart	Question grid	Gathering grid	Time line
Story map	Sequence chart	Topic list		

High-Quality Models

Each core unit in the print book and in the **Net-text** begins with a high-interest model, complete with annotations pointing out key features. Once students have read and analyzed each model, they will be ready—and excited—to begin their own writing. Other models and examples throughout each unit offer specific techniques that students can use in their own writing.

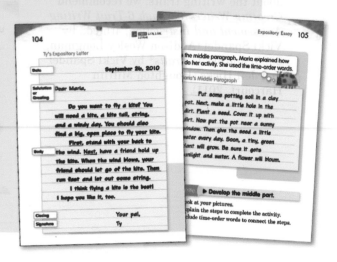

Individual Writing

Write Source print and technology resources make it easy for writing-workshop students to work on their own. They also provide specific help whenever students have questions about their writing. Here are some of the areas that are addressed:

- catching the reader's interest
- providing background information
- developing strong paragraphs
- elaborating (adding facts, examples, anecdotes, etc.)
- organizing ideas by time and location
- quoting
- using transitions
- drawing conclusions
- calling the reader to act

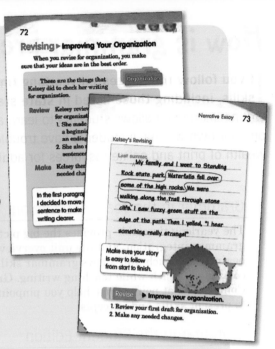

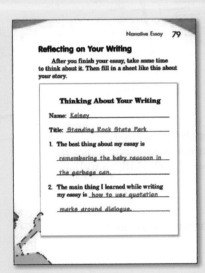

Peer and Teacher Response

Write Source teaches peer responding and provides a peer response sheet. Consistent integration of the traits into the writing process allows students and teachers to speak a common language as they conduct response sessions. Traits-based checklists help pinpoint just what is working—and what could work better—in each piece of writing.

Whole-Class Sharing

Write Source helps students prepare their work for whole-class sharing— whether in a traditional presentation or in the public section of the Online Portfolio. In addition, the program provides a wealth of suggestions for publishing in a variety of forms and for a variety of audiences.

How is grammar presented?

If you follow the suggested yearlong timetable, you will cover all the key grammar skills, including those listed in state standards. Grammar instruction integrated into writing instruction allows students to learn about grammar in context when they are working on their own writing. If students have trouble with a particular concept, you can refer to a wealth of print and online resources for additional support.

Grammar in the Teacher's Edition

The yearlong timetable provides the big picture of grammar integration, and the unit overview at the beginning of each unit shows grammar skills and concepts to teach while teaching writing. Grammar Connections at point of use help you pinpoint the time to present skills and concepts.

Grammar in the Student Edition

Forms of Writing

In each core forms of writing unit, grammar instruction is integrated into the revising and editing steps. Grammar instruction includes examples, practice, and application activities, and it links to students' writing.

Basic Grammar and Writing

For more grammar in the context of writing, refer to "Working with Words" and "Building Sentences." Use these minilessons to teach specific grammar and style topics that students can apply to their writing. These pages include examples of each skill, as well as practice activities.

Proofreader's Guide

This unit serves as a complete conventions guide, providing grammar, usage, and mechanics rules, instruction, examples, and practice.

Grammar in Other Program Components

The *SkillsBook* provides more than 130 grammar, usage, punctuation, mechanics, spelling, and sentence-construction activities. For key topics at each grade, GrammarSnap provides interactive instruction, practice, and basic skills reinforcement through videos, minilessons, games, and quizzes. The *Assessment* book contains a pretest, benchmark tests, and a post-test for basic writing and editing skills. *Daily Language Workouts* includes a year's worth of sentences (daily) and paragraphs (weekly) for editing practice.

Planning Grammar Instruction

Should I implement all of the suggested basic grammar activities?

In the course of the year, if you assigned every grammar exercise listed in the unit scope and sequence charts (located in the unit overviews of your Teacher's Edition), your students would complete **all** of the "Basic Grammar and Writing," "Proofreader's Guide," *SkillsBook*, and GrammarSnap activities.

Because the most effective teaching of grammar happens in context, grammar instruction appears at appropriate times during the revising and editing steps of the core writing forms units. As the teacher, you must choose the type and amount that will best meet the needs of your students.

How are all the grammar resources related?

The *SkillsBook* grammar activities parallel and expand on the rules and exercises found in the "Proofreader's Guide." In "Basic Grammar and Writing," brief exercises function well as minilessons and may be assigned on an as-needed basis. GrammarSnap offers additional support for key grammar topics in an engaging, interactive format.

How do I use the unit scope and sequence charts?

The sample below from the persuasive writing unit is followed by an explanation of how to read and use the charts.

Persuasive Writing Overview **126B**

Suggested Persuasive Writing Unit (Four Weeks)

Day	Writing and Skills Instruction	Student Edition		SkillsBook	Daily Language Workouts	Write Source Online
		Persuasive Writing Unit	Resource Units*			
1–5	**Persuasive Paragraph: A Class Need** (Model, Prewriting, Writing, Revising, Editing) ⬤ Literature Connections *Saving Money*	128–135			34–35, 94	*Interactive Whiteboard Lessons*
	Skills Activities:					
	• Pronouns		334, 462–463	127–128		GrammarSnap
	• Fragments		356, 449 (+)	103–104		GrammarSnap
opt.	*Giving Speeches*	304–305				
	Persuasive Essay: A Persuasive	126–139			36–37, 95	

1. The Resource Units column indicates the Student Edition pages that cover rules, examples, and exercises for corresponding skills activities.
2. The *SkillsBook, Daily Language Workouts,* and Write Source Online columns indicate pages and information from those particular resources.

How do I use *Daily Language Workouts*?

Daily Language Workouts is a teacher resource that provides a high-interest sentence for each day of the year and weekly paragraphs for additional editing and proofreading practice. This regular practice helps students develop the objectivity they need to effectively edit their own writing.

How is writing across the curriculum addressed?

Write Source provides a wide variety of writing-across-the-curriculum activities and assignments. It promotes *writing to show learning, writing to learn new concepts,* and *writing to reflect on learning.*

Writing to Show Learning

Writing to show learning is the most common type of writing that content-area teachers assign. The following forms of writing covered in the program are commonly used for this purpose.

- descriptive paragraph and essay
- narrative paragraph and essay
- expository paragraph and essay
- persuasive paragraph and essay
- response paragraph and book review
- response to a poem
- research report

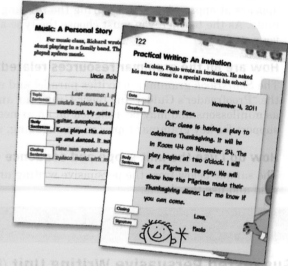

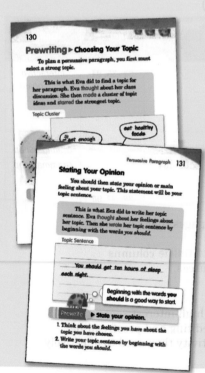

Sample Writing-Across-the-Curriculum Assignments

Descriptive Writing
Science or Math: A Shape Riddle

Narrative Writing
Social Studies: A Community Helper
Music: A Personal Story

Expository Writing
Science: An Animal Report

Persuasive Writing
Science: Endangered Animal Paragraph
Social Studies: Flier for an Event

How does *Write Source* teach academic vocabulary?

*W*rite Source gives students the opportunity to learn and use academic vocabulary so essential for success in school.

Academic Vocabulary in Write Source

Academic vocabulary refers to the words students must know in order to understand the concepts they encounter in school. Academic vocabulary terms such as *process, create, review,* and *compare* are not specific to any one subject but rather denote key ideas and skills relevant to many subject areas. In a sense, academic vocabulary is the language of school. To be successful in school, students must understand and be able to use academic vocabulary as they write about and discuss what they learn in class.

The *Write Source* Academic Vocabulary feature gives students the opportunity to learn and practice using new academic vocabulary in a collaborative activity. This feature, which appears at the beginning of each unit of the Student Edition, provides a brief explanation of each academic vocabulary word, followed by a prompt that motivates students to practice using the term.

- Academic vocabulary is taken from words appearing in the unit.
- Students work with a partner to read the explanations of the academic vocabulary.
- Each explanation is accompanied by an activity or question that prompts students to demonstrate their understanding of the word.

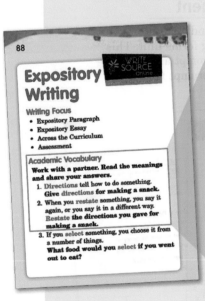

Academic Vocabulary

Work with a partner. Read the meanings and share your answers.

1. **Directions** tell how to do something. **Give directions for making a snack.**

2. When you **restate** something, you say it again, or you say it in a different way. **Restate the directions you gave for making a snack.**

How is test preparation covered?

Each core forms of writing unit in the Student Edition prepares students for responding to testing prompts. **If students complete their work in each of the core units, they will have learned the skills necessary for success on any type of writing assessment.** Here are some of the main features in the Student Edition that address testing.

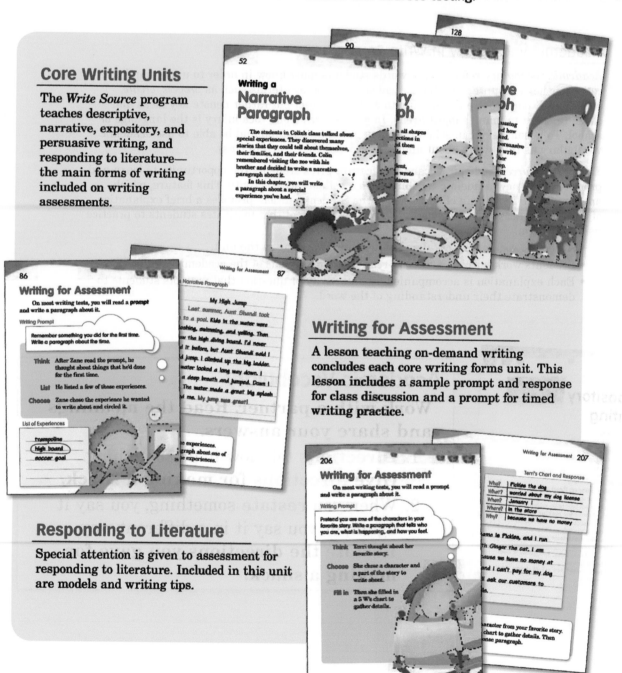

Core Writing Units

The *Write Source* program teaches descriptive, narrative, expository, and persuasive writing, and responding to literature— the main forms of writing included on writing assessments.

Writing for Assessment

A lesson teaching on-demand writing concludes each core writing forms unit. This lesson includes a sample prompt and response for class discussion and a prompt for timed writing practice.

Responding to Literature

Special attention is given to assessment for responding to literature. Included in this unit are models and writing tips.

Taking Classroom Tests

The chapter on test taking includes a section entitled "Short-Answer Test" that models how to restate the question information when writing an answer.

Writing Across the Curriculum

The writing-across-the-curriculum assignments at the end of the core writing units help students prepare for on-demand writing in content-based tests.

Test Prep for Grammar Skills

Tests at the end of each section in the "Proofreader's Guide" follow a standardized test format. Familiarity with this formatting will help students do their best on tests of writing ability.

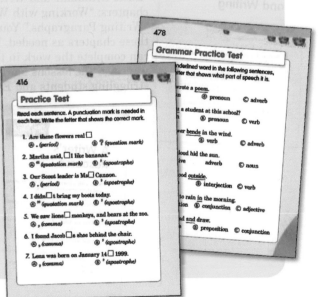

How is differentiation handled in the Student Edition?

Write Source texts, by design, **provide differentiation** in writing instruction—from struggling learners and English-language learners to advanced, independent students.

Core Forms of Writing Units

Options for implementation: You can implement the forms of writing units, one assignment after another, as delineated in the yearlong timetable (pages TE-32–TE-35), helping individuals or small groups of students as needed. Or you can differentiate instruction in any number of ways. Here are three of the many possibilities:

- Have **struggling learners** focus on the single-paragraph writing assignment in each unit while other students complete the multiparagraph essay assignment.
- Have **advanced learners** work individually or in small groups on the multiparagraph composition assignment in each unit, while you guide struggling learners step by step through the development of the composition.
- Conduct a **writing workshop** (pages TE-20–TE-21), asking students to develop one or more assignments in a unit at their own pace.

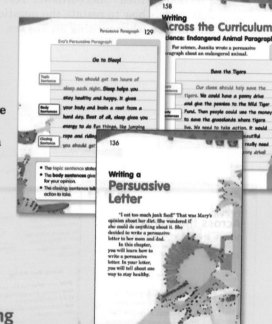

Basic Grammar and Writing

"Basic Grammar and Writing" covers the basics in three chapters: "Working with Words," "Building Sentences," and "Writing Paragraphs." You can differentiate instruction with these chapters as needed. For example, advanced students can complete the work in these chapters independently while you cover the lessons more carefully and selectively with struggling students and English language learners.

A Writer's Resource

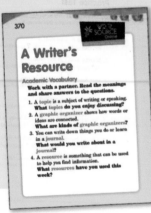

Advanced students can find their own answers to writing questions in this section, while you can find minilesson ideas for struggling learners and English language learners with specific writing needs.

How is differentiation handled in the Teacher's Edition?

The Teacher's Edition provides point-of-use differentiation for struggling learners, English language learners, and advanced learners.

Struggling Learners

The Struggling Learners notes allow you to customize lessons to meet the needs of students who may have difficulty completing the work. These notes provide alternative approaches, extra practice, or additional insights.

Struggling Learners

Many students may not play an instrument yet and may also have difficulty generating ideas about listening to music. Modify the **Before You Write** activity by making a cluster like the one shown on the page. In the center, write "listening to music." Add details by prompting students to offer the following:

- a song that makes them think of a special time
- how a piece of (or certain kind of) music makes them feel
- places they listen to music
- what kind of music they like the most
- songs they like to sing or dance to

English Language Learners

Students have a much larger range of words and phrases to describe their feelings in their first language. Distribute a photocopy of the reproducible T-Chart (TE page 503) and have students list these words and phrases in the left column.

Then ask students to explain when they would feel the way these words describe and help students to translate the words into English. Have them write the English equivalents in the right column to refer to as they write.

English Language Learners

The English Language Learners notes help you to guide students with limited language skills through the lessons. These notes provide extra practice, alternative approaches, connections to first languages, glossaries of new terms, demonstration ideas, and more.

Advanced Learners

The Advanced Learners notes help you enhance the lessons for students who need to be challenged. Some of the notes extend the lessons; others take advanced students beyond the page.

Advanced Learners

Challenge students to respond to Mary's letter by writing a friendly letter to Mary from her parents. Have them include the following:

- her parents' opinion
- reasons they agree or disagree with Mary

- what they plan to buy at the grocery store

Have students compare their letters and the reasons they used.

What research supports the *Write Source* program?

Write Source reflects the best thinking and research on writing instruction.

Applying the Process Approach to Writing

Research: The process approach, discussed by educators Donald M. Murray and Donald H. Graves, among others, breaks writing down into a series of steps—prewriting through publishing. Research has shown that students write more effectively and thoughtfully if they approach their work as a process rather than as an end product.

Graves, Donald. H. *Writing: Teachers and Children at Work*. Heinemann, 2003.

Murray, Donald. M.; Newkirk, Thomas; Miller, Lisa C. *The Essential Don Murray: Lessons from America's Greatest Writing Teacher*. Boynton/Cook Heinemann, 2009.

Write Source: All writing units and assignments are arranged according to the steps in the writing process. This arrangement helps students manage their work, especially in the case of longer essay or research report assignments.

Sequencing Assignments

Research: Writing instructor and researcher James Moffett developed a sequence of writing assignments—known as the "universe of discourse"—that has over the years served countless English/language arts classrooms. Moffett sequences the modes of writing according to their connection or immediacy to the writer. Moffett suggests that students first develop descriptive and narrative pieces because the students have an immediate, personal connection to this type of writing. Next, they should develop informational pieces that require some investigation before moving on to more challenging, reflective writing, such as persuasive essays and position papers.

Moffett, James. *Teaching the Universe of Discourse*. Boynton/Cook, 1987.

Related Title: Fleischer, Cathy; Andrew-Vaughn, Sarah. *Writing Outside Your Comfort Zone: Helping Students Navigate Unfamiliar Genres*. Heinemann, 2009.

Write Source: The writing units and assignments in the *Write Source* texts are arranged according to the "universe of discourse," starting with descriptive and narrative writing, moving on to expository writing, and so on. These assignments are designed to be used in a sequence that supports an existing writing curriculum or integrated reading/language arts program.

Implementing a Writing Workshop

Research: Countless respected writing instructors and researchers have advocated the importance of establishing a community of writers in the classroom. Teachers can establish such a community by implementing a writing workshop. In a writing workshop, students are immersed in all aspects of writing, including sharing their work with their peers.

Atwell, Nancie. *In the Middle: New Understandings About Writing, Reading, and Learning.* Heinemann, 1998.

Write Source: The instruction in *Write Source* is clearly presented so that most students can work independently on their writing in a workshop. In addition, the core forms of writing units contain innumerable opportunities for workshop minilessons.

Producing Writing with Detail

Research: Rebekah Caplan learned through her teaching experience that students don't automatically know how to add details to their personal, informational, and persuasive writing. She discovered with her students that adding detail to writing is a skill that must be practiced regularly. To address this problem, Caplan came up with the "show-me" sentence strategy, in which students begin with a basic idea—"My locker is messy"—and create a brief paragraph that shows rather than tells the idea.

Caplan, Rebekah. *Writers in Training: A Guide to Developing a Composition Program.* Dale Seymour Publications, 1984.

Related Title: Bernabi, Gretchen S.; Hover, Jayne; Candler, Cynthia. *Crunchtime: Lessons to Help Students Blow the Roof Off Writing Tests—and Become Better Writers in the Process.* Heinemann, 2009.

Write Source: *Daily Language Workouts* contains a series of show-me sentences that teachers can implement as a regular classroom warm-up.

Meeting Students' Diverse Needs

Research: Many students in today's classrooms struggle with writing. For struggling students, following the writing process is not enough. According to the research done by James L. Collins, struggling students need specific strategies and aids to help them become better writers. Collins found that these students benefit from skills instruction integrated into the process of writing, color coding and signposts in the presentation of instructional material, the use of graphic organizers, instructions presented in discreet chunks of copy, and so on.

Collins, James L. *Strategies for Struggling Writers.* Guilford Press, 1998.

Related Title: Cruz, M. Colleen; Calkins, Lucy. *A Quick Guide to Reaching Struggling Writers, K–5.* FirstHand/Heinemann, 2008.

Write Source: The core writing forms units contain all the key features from Collins's work. As a result, the units are well suited to struggling learners and English language learners.

Yearlong Timetable

This suggested yearlong timetable presents **one possible sequence** of writing and language skills units based on a five-days-per-week writing class. A logical sequence of units and lessons is built into the timetable. This logical sequence, progressing from personal to more challenging forms, supports an existing writing curriculum or integrated reading/language arts program.

First Quarter

Week	Writing Lessons	Write Source	Grammar and Writing Skills
1	Getting Started Why Write?	TE-76 and 580–583* 1	
2	Using the Writing Process Writing in Journals and Learning Logs	4–5 306–309	**Skills Assessments** Pretests: Using the Right Word
3	One Writer's Process	6–15	**Skills Assessments** Pretests: Punctuation, Editing for Mechanics
	Working with a Partner	16–19	
	Learning to Listen	316–317	
4	Traits of Good Writing	20–27	**Skills Assessments** Pretests: Understanding Sentences, Parts of Speech
	Using a Rubric	28–31	
5	Writing Paragraphs	364–369	End punctuation, fragments, complete sentences
6	Writing a Descriptive Paragraph (Model, Prewriting, Writing, Revising, Editing)	40–45	Adjectives, common and proper nouns
7	Descriptive Writing Across the Curriculum	46–47	Pronouns, capitalization
	Practical Writing: An E-Mail Message	48–49	
8	Writing a Narrative Paragraph (Model, Prewriting, Writing, Revising, Editing)	52–57	Adjectives, verbs (action), prepositions
	Publishing and Portfolios	32–37	
	Taking Tests	318–323	
9	Writing a Narrative Essay (Model, Prewriting)	58–63	

*All remaining page numbers in the timetable refer to the Student Edition.

Second Quarter

Week	Writing Lessons	Write Source	Grammar and Writing Skills
1	**Writing a Narrative Essay** (Writing)	64–69	Quotation marks, punctuating dialogue, complete sentences
2	**Narrative Essay** *(cont.)* (Revising)	70–75	Verb (tenses), adjectives
	Working with a Partner	16–19	
3	**Narrative Essay** *(cont.)* (Editing, Publishing, Reflecting)	76–81	End punctuation, capitalization, spelling (plurals), contractions
	Narrative Writing for Assessment	86–87	
	Giving Speeches *(opt.)*	304–305	
4	**Writing a Response Paragraph** (Model, Prewriting, Writing, Revising, Editing)	166–171	Punctuating titles, capitalization
	Book Review for Fiction (Model, Prewriting)	172–175	
5	**Fiction Review** *(cont.)* (Writing, Revising, Editing, Publishing, Reflecting)	176–183	Sentence combining, punctuating titles, end punctuation, spelling
6	**Writing an Expository Paragraph** (Model, Prewriting, Writing, Revising, Editing)	90–95	Kinds of sentences, end punctuation
7	**Writing an Expository Essay** (Model, Prewriting, Writing)	96–107	
8	**Expository Essay** *(cont.)* (Revising)	108–113	Kinds of sentences, common and proper nouns, adverbs, verbs (irregular)
	Working with a Partner	16–19	
9	**Expository Essay** *(cont.)* (Editing, Publishing, Reflecting)	114–119	Commas in a series, capitalization, subject-verb agreement, commas
	Giving Speeches	304–305	
	Expository Writing for Assessment	124–125	

Third Quarter

Week	Writing Lessons	Write Source	Grammar and Writing Skills
1	**Writing a Persuasive Paragraph** (Model, Prewriting, Writing, Revising, Editing)	128–135	Pronouns, fragments
	Viewing and Listening Skills	310–315	
2	**Writing a Persuasive Letter** (Model, Prewriting)	136–141	
3	**Persuasive Letter** *(cont.)* (Writing, Revising)	142–149	Adjectives to compare, verbs, nouns (possessive)
	Working with Partners	16–19	
4	**Persuasive Letter** *(cont.)* (Editing, Publishing, Reflecting)	150–157	Commas (in dates and addresses), capitalization, abbreviations, mechanics review, spelling
	Persuasive Writing for Assessment	162–163	Commas
	Giving Speeches *(opt.)*	304–305	
5	**Writing Across the Curriculum** Teacher's Choice (Narrative—A Community Helper, Personal Music Story; Expository—Animal Report, Invitation; Persuasive—Endangered Animal, Event Flier)	82–85 120–123 158–161	
6	**Comparing Two Fiction Books** (Model, Prewriting, Writing, Revising, Editing, Publishing)	194–197	Pronouns, verbs, punctuating titles, apostrophes (to show possession)
	Comparing Two Fiction Books *(cont.)*	198–199	
7	**Response Writing for Assessment**	206–207	
	Giving Speeches *(opt.)*	304–305	
8	**Writing Add-On Stories** (Model, Prewriting)	210–215	
9	**Add-On Stories** *(cont.)* (Writing, Revising, Editing, Publishing)	216–225	Punctuating dialogue, prepositions, conjunctions, interjections, subject-verb agreement, punctuation review
	Working with Partners	16–19	

Fourth Quarter

Week	Writing Lessons	Write Source	Grammar and Writing Skills
1	**Writing Poems: Rhyming Poem** (Model, Prewriting, Writing, Revising, Editing, Publishing)	242–250	Adjectives, antonyms, parts of speech review, spelling
2	**Name Poem and Other Kinds of Poems** (ABC Poem, Tongue Twister, Shape Poem, Terse Verse, Diamond Poem, 5 W's Poem)	251–255	
	Responding to a Poem (Model, Prewriting)	200–203	
3	**Responding to a Poem** (cont.) (Writing, Revising, Editing, Publishing)	204–205	Nouns, punctuating titles, commas in compound sentences
	Book Review of a Nonfiction Book (Model, Prewriting, Writing)	184–189	
4	**Nonfiction Review** (cont.) (Revising, Editing, Publishing)	191–193	Plurals, using the right word, commas (after introductory words), capitalization
	Finding Information	258–271	
5	**Writing a Research Report** (Model, Prewriting)	272–281	
6	**Research Report** (cont.) (Writing, Revising)	282–289	Sentence variety, pronouns (possessive), nouns (possessive), capitalization review, rambling sentences, comma review, subject-verb agreement
	Working with a Partner	16–19	
7	**Research Report** (cont.) (Editing, Publishing, Reflecting)	290–293	Spelling review
	Creating a Multimedia Presentation (Prewriting, Writing, Revising, Editing, Publishing) (opt.)	294–297	
8	**Creating a Play** (Model, Prewriting)	226–231	
9	**Creating a Play** (cont.) (Writing, Revising, Editing, Publishing) Journal and Portfolio Review Final Reflection Essay	232–241	Pronouns, using the right word, spelling

Reading-Writing Connection

The literary works listed on pages TE-36–TE-43 provide high-interest **mentor texts** that you can use to inspire your students as you teach the different forms of writing. Use these texts to accentuate **writer's craft**:

- Read **strong beginnings** or **strong endings** to inspire students as they create their own beginnings and endings.
- Read paragraphs that **elaborate ideas** or demonstrate **strong organization**.
- Read from two different examples to **contrast voice** and **word choice**.
- Read from different authors to examine their **sentence fluency**.

Narrative Books for Grades 1–2

First Year Letters
Julie Danneberg, 2003

My Great-Aunt Arizona
Gloria Houston, 1997

Fireflies
Julie Brinckloe, 1986

I Know a Lady
Charlotte Zolotow, 1992

The Relatives Came
Cynthia Rylant, 2005

Owl Moon
Jane Yolen, 1987

Something Beautiful
Sharon Dennis Wyeth, 2002

The Wednesday Surprise
Eve Bunting, 1989

Apple Picking Time
Michele B. Slawson, 1998

A Chair for My Mother
Vera B. Williams, 1982

All the Places to Love
Patricia MacLachlan, 1994

Icy Watermelon/ Sandía Fría
Mary Sue Galindo, 2008

Bravo, Amelia Bedelia!
Herman Parish, 1997

Mama Played Baseball
David A. Adler, 2003

Uptown
Bryan Collier, 2007

Marianthe's Story: Painted Words and Spoken Memories
Aliki, 1998

Uncle Andy's: A Faabbbulous Visit with Andy Warhol
James Warhola, 2003

Alexander and the Terrible, Horrible, No Good, Very Bad Day
Judith Viorst, 1972

The Listening Walk
Paul Showers, 1991

There's an Alligator Under My Bed
Mercer Mayer, 1987

If I Could Drive a Fire Truck!
Michael Teitelbaum, Uldis Klavins,
Jeff Walker, 2001

I Took My Frog to the Library
Eric A. Kimmel, 1992

My Daddy is a Soldier
Kirk Hilbrecht, 2000

The Gardener
Sarah Stewart, 1997

Mr. Yee Fixes Cars
Alice K. Flanagan, 1998

Pen Pals
Joan Holub, 1997

Junie B. Jones and the Stupid Smelly Bus
Barbara Park, 1992

My First Kwanzaa
Karen Katz, 2003

The Hello, Goodbye Window
Norton Juster, 2005

Music, Music for Everyone
Vera B. Williams, 1988

Wash Day
Barbara H. Cole, 2004

The Cool Crazy Crickets
David Elliott, 2001

The Day I Had to Play With My Sister
Crosby Bonsall, 1999

Fishing Day
Andrea Davis Pinkney, 2003

Red Rubber Boot Day
Mary Lyn Ray, 2000

My Day in the Garden
Miela Ford, 1999

Harry Gets an Uncle
Barbara Ann Porte, 2002

Show & Tell Day
Anne Rockwell, 2000

I Live in Brooklyn
Mari Takabayashi, 2004

Charlie and Lola:
Snow is My Favorite and My Best
Lauren Child, 2006

Expository Books for Grades 1–2

Planting a Rainbow
Lois Ehlert, 1992

My Five Senses
Aliki, 1989

Sleep is for Everyone
Paul Showers, 1997

Air Is All Around You
Franklyn M. Branley, 2006

Animals in Winter
Henrietta Bancroft and
Richard G. Van Gelder, 1997

Sounds All Around
Wendy Pfeffer, 1995

What Makes a Shadow?
Clyde Robert Bulla, 1994

The Furry News: How to Make a Newspaper
Loreen Leedy, 1993

How to Make a Rainbow: Great Things to Make and Do for 7 Year Olds
Deborah Manley, 1994

Watch Me Make a Bird Feeder
Jack Otten, 2002

Watch Me Build a Sandcastle
Jack Otten, 2002

Watch Me Plant a Garden
Jack Otten, 2002

Watch Me Make a Mask
Jack Otten, 2002

Watch Me Make a Birthday Card
Jack Otten, 2002

Let's Make Tacos
Mary Hill, 2002

Let's Make Pizza
Mary Hill, 2002

Let's Make Cookies
Mary Hill, 2002

I Can Play Games: Fun-to-Play Games for Younger Children
Petra Boase, 2000

Let's Jump Rope
Sarah Hughes, 2000

Let's Play Hopscotch
Sarah Hughes, 2000

Let's Play Jacks
Sarah Hughes, 2000

Let's Play Tag
Sarah Hughes, 2000

Let's Play Hide-And-Seek
Sarah Hughes, 2000

How High Can a Dinosaur Count?: And Other Math Mysteries
Valorie Fisher, 2006

I Face the Wind
Vicki Cobb, 2004

Arrowhawk
Lola M. Schaefer, 2004

Garden of the Spirit Bear
Dorothy Hinshaw Patent, 2004

Pupniks: The Story of Two Space Dogs
S. Ruth Lubka, 2004

They Call Me Woolly: What Animal Names Can Tell Us
Keith DuQuette, 2002

Brrr: A Book About Polar Animals
Melvin & Gilda Berger, 2001

Flotsam
David Wiesner, 2006

Water Hole
Zahavit Shalev, 2005

Octopuses
Lola M. Schaefer, 2006

Bug Faces
Darlyne A. Murawski, 2000

An Island Grows
Lola M. Schaefer, 2006

What Do You Do with a Tail Like This?
Steve Jenkins and Robin Page, 2003

My Family Plays Music
Judy Cox, 2003

On the Go
Ann Morris, 1994

Houses and Homes
Ann Morris, 1995

Me on the Map
Joan Sweeney, 1996

Persuasive Books for Grades 1-2

I Wanna Iguana
Karen Kaufman Orloff, 2004

Dear Mrs. La Rue: Letters From Obedience School
Mark Teague, 2004

Dear Mr. Blueberry
Simon James, 1996

Don't Take Your Snake for a Stroll
Karin Ireland, 2003

The Perfect Pet
Margie Palatini, 2003

Maybe You Should Fly a Jet! Maybe You Should Be a Vet!
Theo LeSieg, 2001

Take Care Of Your Teeth
Don L. Curry, 2005

Take Care Of Your Eyes
Don L. Curry, 2004

The Great Kapok Tree: A Tale of the Amazon Rain Forest
Lynne Cherry, 2001

Priscilla and the Pink Planet
Nathaniel Hobbie, 2004

Go Away, Dog
Joan L. Nodset, 1999

Cows Can't Fly
David Milgrim, 2000

Allie's Basketball Dream
Barbara E. Barber, 1998

Grandpa's Corner Store
DyAnne DiSalvo-Ryan, 2000

Bernelly & Harriet: The Country Mouse and the City Mouse
Elizabeth Dahlie, 2002

Hundred Million Reasons for Owning an Elephant: (Or at Least a Dozen I Can Think of Right Now)
Lois G. Grambling, 1990

The Environment (The Reason Why Series)
Irving Adler, Peggy Adler, 1976

Why Should I Eat Well? (Why Should I? Books)
Claire Llewellyn, 2005

Fruits Are Fun
Amanda Rondeau, 2002

Why Should I Eat This Carrot?
Angela Royston, 2004

Drink More Water
Cindy Devine Dalton, 2000

Bengal Tiger (Save Our Animals)
Richard Spilsbury, 2007

Asian Elephant (Save Our Animals)
Richard Spilsbury, 2007

Operation Turtle (Save Our Species)
Jill Bailey, 1992

Rainforests (Save Our World)
Jane Parker, 1999

Books About Responding to Literature for Grades 1–2

Alexander and the Terrible, Horrible, No Good, Very Bad Day
Judith Viorst, 1972

The Hello, Goodbye Window
Norton Juster, 2005

The Stories Julian Tells
Ann Cameron, 1989

Get Ready for Second Grade, Amber Brown
Paula Danziger, 2003

The Case of the Spooky Sleepover (Jigsaw Jones Mystery)
James Preller, 2001

The New Girl . . . and Me
Jacqui Robbins, 2006

How I Became a Pirate
Melinda Long, 2003

Henry and Mudge: The First Book
Cynthia Rylant, 1996

Mr. George Baker
Amy Hest, 2004

Ready, Freddy!: Don't Sit on My Lunch
Abby Klein, 2005

A Fine, Fine School
Sharon Creech, 2001

Why Do Leaves Change Color?
Betsy Maestro, 1994

And So They Build
Bert Kitchen, 1995

Bottle Houses: The Creative World of Grandma Prisbrey
Melissa Eskridge Slaymaker, 2004

Snakes! Strange and Wonderful
Laurence Pringle, 2004

Bill Pickett: Rodeo-Ridin' Cowboy
Andrea Pinkney, 1999

Sunken Treasure
Gail Gibbons, 1990

Welcome to the Green House
Jane Yolen

Welcome to the Ice House
Jane Yolen

Alexander and the Wind-Up Mouse
Leo Lionni

The 20th Century Children's Poetry Treasury
Jack Prelutsky, 1999

Kids Pick the Funniest Poems
Bruce Lansky

I Like This Poem
Kaye Webb, 1999

Shadows and Reflections
Tana Hoban, 1990

Books About Creative Writing for Grades 1–2

The Kingfisher Treasury of Animal Stories
Jane Olliver, 1992

The Very Hungry Caterpillar
Eric Carle, 1994

Guess How Much I Love You
Sam McBratney, 1996

Click, Clack, Moo: Cows That Type
Doreen Cronin, Betsy Lewin, 2003

Frog and Toad Together
Arnold Lobel, 1999

Henny Penny
Vivian French, 2006

The Bremen-Town Musicians
Ilse Plume, 1998

Stone Soup
Marcia Brown, 1999

There Was an Old Lady Who Swallowed a Fly
Simms Taback, 1997

Gingerbread Baby
Jan Brett, 1999

Forecasting Fun: Weather Nursery Rhymes
Paula Knight, Melissa Carpenter, 2004

The Kingfisher Book of Nursery Tales
Terry Pierce, 2004

The Best Hawaiian Style Mother Goose Ever! Hawai'i's Version of 14 Very Popular Verses
Kevin Sullivan, 1995

The Neighborhood Mother Goose
Nina Crews, 2003

Mother Goose Rhyme Time People
Kimberly Faurot, 2006

"I Did It Because...": How a Poem Happens
Loris Lesynski, 2006

Grasshopper Pie and Other Poems: All Aboard Poetry Reader
David Steinberg, 2004

Chanting Rhymes (First Verses Series)
John Foster, 1998

Read A Rhyme, Write A Rhyme
Jack Prelutsky, 2005

Busy Buzzing Bumblebees and Other Tongue Twisters (An I Can Read Book)
Alvin Schwartz, 1992

Creepy Crawly Critters and Other Halloween Tongue Twisters
Nola Buck, 1996

The Kingfisher Book of Children's Poetry
Michael Rosen, 1993

Doodle Dandies: Poems That Take Shape
J. Patrick Lewis, 2002

Hippopotamus Stew and Other Silly Animal Poems
Joan Horton, 2006

The Kingfisher Book of Family Poems
Belinda Hollyer, 2003

Reference Books for Grades 1–2

The American Heritage First Dictionary
Edited by Editors of The American Heritage Dictionaries, 2006

The World Almanac for Kids 2007
Editors of World Almanac, 2006

Kingfisher First Encyclopedia of Animals
Editors of Kingfisher, 2005

Kingfisher First Thesaurus
George Beal, Martin Chatterton, 2004

The Kingfisher First Encyclopedia
Editors of Kingfisher, 2005

First Nature Encyclopedia
DK Publishing, 2006

Look-it-up: Animals On The Move
Gallimard Jeunesse, 2002

Look-it-up: Baby Animals In The Wild
Gallimard Jeunesse, 2002

Look-it-up: Animal Homes
Gallimard Jeunesse, 2002

Birds (Kingfisher Young Knowledge)
Nicola Davies, 2003

Smithsonian Kids' Field Guides: Birds of North America West
DK Publishing, 2001

Parrots and Parakeets As Pets (A True Book)
Elaine Landau, 1998

Complete Library Skills (Grade K–2)
School Specialty Publishing, 2004

"L" Is for Library
Sonya Terry, 2006

A Day in the Life of a Librarian (First Facts)
Judy Monroe, 2004

Scope and Sequence

Skills taught and/or reviewed in the *Write Source* program, grades K–8, are featured in the following scope and sequence chart.

FORMS OF WRITING

	Grades K	1	2	3	4	5	6	7	8
Narrative Writing									
sentences	●	●							
paragraph	●	●	●	●	●	●	●	●	●
narrative prompts		●	●	●	●	●	●	●	●
narrative essay			●	●	●	●	●	●	●
phase autobiography								●	●
Expository Writing									
sentences	●	●							
paragraph	●	●	●	●	●	●	●	●	●
expository prompts	●	●	●	●	●	●	●	●	●
expository essay			●	●	●	●	●	●	●
classification essay									
cause-and-effect essay								●	
comparison-contrast essay								●	●
Persuasive Writing									
sentences		●							
paragraph	●	●	●	●	●	●	●	●	●
persuasive prompts			●	●	●	●	●	●	●
persuasive letter			●	●	●	●	●	●	●
persuasive essay			●	●	●	●	●	●	●
editorial								●	●
problem-solution essay							●	●	●
personal commentary								●	
position essay									●
Response to Literature									
sentences	●								
paragraph	●	●	●	●	●	●	●	●	●
response prompts	●	●	●	●	●	●	●	●	●
book review	●	●	●	●	●	●	●	●	●
journal response				●	●	●	●	●	●
response to literature							●	●	●
letter to an author									●
theme analysis									●

	K	1	2	3	4	5	6	7	8
Descriptive Writing									
sentences	■	■							
paragraph		■	■	■	■	■	■	■	■
descriptive essay			■	■	■	■	■	■	■
descriptive prompts				■	■	■			
Creative Writing									
poetry		■	■	■	■	■	■	■	■
story	■	■	■	■	■	■	■	■	■
play			■	■	■	■			
Research Writing									
research report		■	■	■	■	■	■	■	■
multimedia presentation			■	■	■	■	■	■	■
summary paragraph			■	■	■	■	■	■	■
Research Skills									
interview an expert		■	■	■	■	■	■	■	■
online research/using the Internet		■	■	■	■	■	■	■	■
understanding the parts of a book		■	■	■	■	■	■	■	■
using a dictionary, a thesaurus, or an encyclopedia		■	■	■	■	■	■	■	■
using diagrams, charts, graphs, and maps		■	■	■	■	■	■	■	■
using reference sources		■	■	■	■	■	■	■	■
using the library		■	■	■	■	■	■	■	■
note taking/summarizing		■	■	■	■	■	■	■	■
using a card catalog			■	■	■	■	■	■	■
using periodicals or magazines			■	■	■	■	■	■	■
using time lines			■	■	■	■	■	■	■
asking questions				■	■	■	■	■	■
bibliography (works cited)				■	■	■	■	■	■
The Tools of Learning									
improving viewing skills		■	■	■	■	■			
interviewing skills		■	■	■	■	■	■		
giving speeches		■	■	■	■	■	■	■	■
journal writing	■	■	■	■	■	■	■	■	■
learning logs		■	■	■	■	■	■	■	■
listening in class	■	■	■	■	■	■	■	■	■
taking classroom tests		■	■	■	■	■	■	■	■
note taking				■	■	■	■	■	■
completing writing assignments							■	■	■

THE WRITING PROCESS Grades

	K	1	2	3	4	5	6	7	8
Prewriting									
Selecting a Topic									
draw pictures	■	■	■						
make lists	■	■	■	■	■	■	■	■	■
sentence starters	■	■	■	■	■	■	■	■	■
chart				■	■	■	■	■	■
cluster			■	■	■	■	■	■	■
brainstorm					■	■	■	■	■
character chart					■	■		■	■
freewrite					■	■	■	■	■
Gathering Details									
drawing	■	■							
story map		■	■	■					
cluster	■	■	■	■	■	■	■	■	■
answer questions	■	■	■	■	■	■	■	■	■
details chart/sheet			■	■	■	■	■	■	■
gathering grid			■	■	■	■	■	■	■
list details/reasons			■	■	■	■	■	■	■
sensory chart	■	■	■	■	■	■	■	■	■
selecting main reasons			■	■	■	■	■	■	■
five W's			■	■	■	■	■	■	■
time line	■			■	■	■	■	■	■
table diagram				■	■	■	■	■	■
opinion statement							■	■	■
counter an objection								■	■
Organizing Details									
time order		■	■	■	■	■	■	■	■
Venn diagram			■	■	■	■	■	■	■
plot chart				■	■	■	■	■	■
time line				■	■	■	■	■	■
note cards				■	■	■	■	■	■
outline ideas				■	■	■	■	■	■
order of importance					■	■	■	■	■
order of location				■	■	■	■	■	
Writing									
topic sentence	■	■	■	■	■	■	■	■	■
opinion statement		■	■	■	■	■	■	■	■
facts, examples	■	■	■	■	■	■	■	■	■
supporting details/reasons		■	■	■	■	■	■	■	■
interesting facts/details			■	■	■	■	■	■	■

	Grades K	1	2	3	4	5	6	7	8
make comparisons			■	■	■	■	■	■	■
dialogue			■	■	■	■	■	■	■
transitions			■	■	■	■	■	■	■
call to action			■	■	■	■	■	■	■
closing sentences			■	■	■	■	■	■	■
final comment/interesting thought			■	■	■	■	■	■	■
focus or thesis statement				■	■	■	■	■	■
action words				■	■	■	■	■	■
direct quotations				■	■	■	■	■	■
sensory details				■	■	■	■	■	■
high point of story				■	■	■	■	■	■
explain theme				■	■	■	■	■	■
reflect on a change, a feeling, an experience, a person				■	■	■	■	■	■
restate opinion/thesis					■	■	■	■	■
summarize					■	■	■	■	■
personal details						■	■	■	■
propose a solution							■	■	■
summarize a problem								■	■
share a new insight								■	■
counter an objection							■	■	■
emphasize a key idea								■	■
point-by-point discussion									■

Revising

Ideas

	Grades K	1	2	3	4	5	6	7	8
sensory details	■	■	■	■	■	■	■	■	■
topic sentence			■	■	■	■	■	■	■
supporting details			■	■	■	■	■	■	■
dialogue				■	■	■	■	■	■
unnecessary details				■	■	■	■	■	■
focus statement					■	■	■	■	■

Organization

	Grades K	1	2	3	4	5	6	7	8
order of ideas/details	■	■	■	■	■	■	■	■	■
transition words		■	■	■	■	■	■	■	■
order of importance			■		■	■	■	■	■
overall organization				■	■	■	■	■	■
order of location				■	■	■	■	■	■
logical order				■	■	■	■	■	■
clear beginning				■	■	■	■	■	■
time order				■	■	■	■	■	■

Revising (Continued)

	Grades K	1	2	3	4	5	6	7	8
Voice									
natural		●	●	●	●	●	●	●	●
convincing				●	●	●	●	●	●
interested				●	●	●	●	●	●
dialogue					●	●	●	●	●
fits audience/purpose					●	●	●	●	●
formal/informal					●	●	●	●	●
knowledgeable					●	●	●	●	●
Word Choice									
sensory words/details	●	●	●	●	●	●	●	●	●
specific nouns			●	●	●	●	●	●	●
action verbs				●	●	●	●	●	●
connotation					●	●	●	●	●
modifiers					●	●	●	●	●
onomatopoeia						●	●	●	●
descriptive words						●	●	●	●
vivid verbs						●	●	●	●
connotation								●	●
Sentence Fluency									
complete sentences		●	●	●	●	●	●	●	●
variety of lengths			●	●	●	●	●	●	●
kinds of sentences			●	●	●	●	●	●	●
combining sentences				●	●	●	●	●	●
compound sentences				●	●	●	●	●	●
complex sentences					●	●	●	●	●
expanded sentences					●	●	●	●	●
variety of beginnings					●	●	●	●	●
types of sentences					●	●	●	●	●
Editing									
capitalization	●	●	●	●	●	●	●	●	●
grammar/punctuation/spelling	●	●	●	●	●	●	●	●	●
proper nouns	●		●	●	●	●	●	●	●
proper adjectives				●	●	●	●	●	●
Publishing									
publish in a variety of ways	●	●	●	●	●	●	●	●	●
review own work to monitor growth		●	●	●	●	●	●	●	●
self- and peer-assessing writing		●	●	●	●	●	●	●	●
use portfolios to save writing		●	●	●	●	●	●	●	●
use published pieces as models for writing	●	●	●	●	●	●	●	●	●

WRITING ACROSS THE CURRICULUM

Grades	K	1	2	3	4	5	6	7	8
Narrative Writing									
reading		■							
music		■	■						
social studies			■			■	■	■	■
practical				■			■	■	■
science				■	■		■	■	■
Expository Writing									
social studies		■		■		■	■	■	■
math		■		■	■	■	■	■	
reading *		■	■	■	■	■	■	■	■
science			■		■		■	■	■
practical				■	■	■	■	■	■
Persuasive Writing									
health		■							
science				■	■	■	■	■	■
social studies				■		■	■	■	■
practical					■	■	■	■	■
math						■		■	■
Descriptive Writing									
math		■	■				■	■	■
science		■	■		■	■	■	■	■
practical				■			■	■	■
social studies					■	■	■	■	■

* The models included in the "Response to Literature" section demonstrate expository writing within the reading curriculum.

GRAMMAR

Understanding Sentences	K	1	2	3	4	5	6	7	8
word order	■	■	■						
declarative	■	■	■	■	■	■	■	■	
exclamatory	■	■	■	■	■	■	■	■	
interrogative	■	■	■	■	■	■	■	■	
complete sentences and fragments	■	■	■	■	■	■	■	■	
simple subjects	■	■	■	■	■	■	■	■	
simple predicates	■	■	■	■	■	■	■	■	
correcting run-on sentences	■	■	■	■	■	■	■	■	
compound			■	■	■	■	■	■	
imperative			■	■	■	■	■	■	
complete predicates				■	■	■	■	■	■

Understanding Sentences (Continued)

	K	1	2	3	4	5	6	7	8
complete subjects				■	■	■	■	■	■
compound predicates				■	■	■	■	■	■
compound subjects				■	■	■	■	■	■
prepositional phrases				■	■	■	■	■	■
appositive phrases					■	■	■	■	■
clauses, dependent and independent					■	■	■	■	■
complex					■	■	■	■	■
modifiers					■	■	■	■	■
noun phrases					■	■	■	■	■
verb phrases					■	■	■	■	■

Using the Parts of Speech

Nouns

	K	1	2	3	4	5	6	7	8
singular and plural		■	■	■	■	■	■	■	■
common/proper		■	■	■	■	■	■	■	■
possessive			■	■	■	■	■	■	■
singular/plural possessive			■	■	■	■	■	■	■
specific				■	■	■	■	■	■
abstract/concrete					■	■	■	■	■
appositives					■	■	■	■	■
collective/compound					■	■	■	■	■
object					■	■	■	■	■
predicate					■	■	■	■	■
subject					■	■	■	■	■
gender					■	■	■	■	■

Verbs

	K	1	2	3	4	5	6	7	8
contractions with *not*		■	■	■	■	■	■	■	■
action	■	■	■	■	■	■	■	■	■
linking		■	■	■	■	■	■	■	■
past tense		■	■	■	■	■	■	■	■
present tense		■	■	■	■	■	■	■	■
subject-verb agreement		■	■	■	■	■	■	■	■
future tense			■	■	■	■	■	■	■
helping			■	■	■	■	■	■	■
singular/plural			■	■	■	■	■	■	■
irregular				■	■	■	■	■	■
simple tense				■	■	■	■	■	■
active/passive voice					■	■	■	■	■
direct objects					■	■	■	■	■
indirect objects					■	■	■	■	■
perfect tense					■	■	■	■	■

	K	1	2	3	4	5	6	7	8
Grades									
transitive/intransitive					■	■	■	■	■
participles						■	■	■	■
continuous tense						■	■	■	■
gerunds							■	■	■
infinitives							■	■	■
Pronouns									
personal		■	■	■	■	■	■	■	■
antecedents		■	■	■	■	■	■	■	■
singular and plural		■	■	■	■	■	■	■	■
possessive		■	■	■	■	■	■	■	■
subject and object			■	■	■	■	■	■	■
demonstrative/interrogative					■	■	■	■	■
gender					■	■	■	■	■
indefinite					■	■	■	■	■
intensive and reflexive					■	■	■	■	■
relative					■	■	■	■	■
Adjectives									
adjectives	■	■	■	■	■	■	■	■	■
comparative/superlative		■	■	■	■	■	■	■	■
articles			■	■	■	■	■	■	■
compound				■	■	■	■	■	■
positive				■	■	■	■	■	■
proper				■	■	■	■	■	■
demonstrative					■	■	■	■	■
equal					■	■	■	■	■
indefinite					■	■	■	■	■
predicate					■	■	■	■	■
Interjections									
interjections		■	■	■	■	■	■	■	■
Adverbs									
of manner				■	■	■	■	■	■
of place	■		■	■	■	■	■	■	■
of time				■	■	■	■	■	■
that modify verbs				■	■	■	■	■	■
of degree					■	■	■	■	■
that modify adjectives and adverbs					■	■	■	■	■
comparative/superlative					■	■	■	■	■
comparing with adverbs					■	■	■	■	■
irregular forms					■	■	■	■	■
positive					■	■	■	■	■

Parts of Speech (Continued)

	K	1	2	3	4	5	6	7	8
Conjunctions									
coordinating			■	■	■	■	■	■	■
correlative					■	■	■	■	■
subordinating					■	■	■	■	■
Prepositions									
prepositions	■		■	■	■	■	■	■	■
prepositional phrases				■	■	■	■	■	■

Mechanics

	K	1	2	3	4	5	6	7	8
Capitalization									
pronoun "I"		■	■	■	■	■		■	■
days, months, holidays		■	■	■	■	■	■	■	■
first words	■	■	■	■	■	■	■	■	■
names of people	■	■	■	■	■	■	■	■	■
proper nouns		■	■	■	■	■	■	■	■
titles used with names		■	■	■	■	■	■	■	■
titles		■	■	■	■	■	■	■	■
beginning of a quotation		■	■	■	■	■	■	■	■
geographic names			■	■	■	■	■	■	■
abbreviations			■	■	■	■	■	■	■
proper adjectives				■	■	■	■	■	■
words used as names			■	■	■	■	■	■	■
names of historical events					■	■	■	■	■
names of religions, nationalities					■	■	■	■	■
organizations					■	■	■	■	■
particular sections of the country					■	■	■	■	■
trade names/official names					■	■	■	■	■
letters to indicate form or direction							■	■	■
specific course names						■	■	■	■
Plurals									
irregular nouns		■	■	■	■	■	■	■	■
most nouns		■	■	■	■	■	■	■	■
nouns ending with *sh, ch, x, s,* and *z*			■	■	■	■	■	■	■
nouns ending in *y*			■	■	■	■	■	■	■
adding '*s*					■	■	■	■	■
compound nouns					■	■	■	■	■
nouns ending with *f* or *fe*					■	■	■	■	■
nouns ending with *ful*					■	■	■	■	■
nouns ending with *o*					■	■	■	■	■

	K	1	2	3	4	5	6	7	8
Abbreviations									
days and months			■	■	■	■	■	■	■
state postal abbreviations				■	■	■	■	■	■
titles of people	■	■	■	■	■	■	■	■	■
addresses			■	■	■	■	■	■	■
acronyms				■	■	■	■	■	■
initialisms				■	■	■	■	■	■
Numbers									
numbers 1 to 9					■	■	■	■	■
numbers only					■	■	■	■	■
sentence beginnings					■	■	■	■	■
very large numbers					■	■	■	■	■
numbers in compound modifiers							■	■	■
time and money							■	■	■
Punctuation									
Periods									
after an initial/an abbreviation		■	■	■	■	■	■	■	■
at the end of a sentence	■	■	■	■	■	■	■	■	■
as a decimal point				■	■	■	■	■	■
after an indirect question							■	■	■
Question Marks									
after questions	■	■	■	■	■	■	■	■	■
after tag questions					■	■	■	■	■
to show doubt					■	■	■	■	■
Exclamation Points									
for words, phrases, and sentences	■	■	■	■	■	■	■	■	■
for interjections			■	■	■	■	■	■	■
Commas									
in a series			■	■	■	■	■	■	■
in dates			■	■	■	■	■	■	■
in friendly letters			■	■	■	■	■	■	■
after introductory words			■	■	■	■	■	■	■
with interjections			■	■	■	■	■	■	■
in a compound sentence				■	■	■	■	■	■
in addresses			■	■	■	■	■	■	■
to set off dialogue			■	■	■	■	■	■	■
in direct address			■	■	■	■	■	■	■
in numbers				■	■	■	■	■	■
to separate equal adjectives				■	■	■	■	■	■

Commas (Continued)	Grades K	1	2	3	4	5	6	7	8
to set off appositives					■	■	■	■	■
to set off interrupters					■	■	■	■	■
to set off phrases					■	■	■	■	■
to set off titles of people							■	■	■
Apostrophes									
in contractions	■	■	■	■	■	■	■	■	■
to form plural possessive nouns			■	■	■	■	■	■	■
to form singular possessive nouns			■	■	■	■	■	■	■
to form some plurals					■	■	■	■	■
to replace omitted numbers/letters					■	■	■	■	■
with indefinite pronouns					■	■	■	■	■
to show shared possession					■	■	■	■	■
in possessives with compound nouns							■	■	■
to express time or amount							■	■	■
Underlining and Italics									
for titles	■	■	■	■	■	■	■	■	■
for special words					■	■	■	■	■
for scientific and foreign words							■	■	■
Quotation Marks									
for direct quotations			■	■	■	■	■	■	■
for titles			■	■	■	■	■	■	■
for special words					■	■	■	■	■
for quotations within a quotation							■	■	■
Colons									
between hour and minutes				■	■	■	■	■	■
in business letters					■	■	■	■	■
to introduce a list of items					■	■	■	■	■
for emphasis							■	■	■
to introduce sentences							■	■	■
Hyphens									
in word division				■	■	■	■	■	■
in compound words					■	■	■	■	■
in fractions					■	■	■	■	■
to create new words					■	■	■	■	■
to join letters and words					■	■	■	■	■
to avoid confusion or awkward spelling							■	■	■
to make adjectives							■	■	■

Grades K 1 2 3 4 5 6 7 8

	K	1	2	3	4	5	6	7	8
Parentheses									
to add information				■	■	■	■	■	■
Dashes									
for emphasis					■	■	■	■	■
to show a sentence break					■	■	■	■	■
to show interrupted speech					■	■	■	■	■
Ellipses									
to show a pause					■	■	■	■	■
to show omitted words					■	■	■	■	■
Semicolons									
in a compound sentence				■	■	■	■	■	■
to separate groups (that have commas) in a series					■	■	■	■	■
with conjunctive adverbs							■	■	■
Usage									
Spelling									
high-frequency words	■	■							
consonant endings				■	■	■	■	■	■
i before *e*				■	■	■	■	■	■
silent *e*				■	■	■	■	■	■
words ending in *y*				■	■	■	■	■	■
Using the Right Word	■		■	■	■	■	■	■	■
Penmanship									
word space, letter space	■	■							
write legibly	■	■	■	■	■	■	■	■	■
margins/spaces				■	■	■	■	■	■

Meeting the Common Core State Standards

The following correlation clearly shows how the *Write Source* program helps students meet grade-specific **Common Core State Standards** for English Language Arts and Literacy in History/Social Studies, Science, and Technical Subjects. The Common Core standards translate their companion **College and Career Readiness standards** into grade-appropriate expectations that students should meet by the end of the school year.

Pages referenced below appear in the Teacher's Edition as well as the Student Edition.

Writing Standards

Text Types and Purposes

College and Career Readiness Standard 1. Write arguments to support claims in an analysis of substantive topics or texts, using valid reasoning and relevant and sufficient evidence.

Grade 2 Standard 1. Write opinion pieces in which they introduce the topic or book they are writing about, state an opinion, supply reasons that support the opinion, use linking words (e.g., because, and, also) to connect opinion and reasons, and provide a concluding statement or section.	**Student Edition pages:** 128–129, 131–132, 133, 137, 138, 140, 141, 142, 143, 146–147, 158, 159, 160, 161, 163, 360–361, 366, 368, 377–378, 387, 395–396 **Net-text:** Persuasive Writing

College and Career Readiness Standard 2. Write informative/explanatory texts to examine and convey complex ideas and information clearly and accurately through the effective selection, organization, and analysis of content.

Grade 2 Standard 2. Write informative/explanatory texts in which they introduce a topic, use facts and definitions to develop points, and provide a concluding statement or section.	**Student Edition pages:** 22, 39, 90–91, 94, 97, 98–99, 100–101, 102–103, 104–107, 109, 110–111, 120–121, 122–123, 126, 142, 161, 173, 176, 178–179, 185, 187, 188–189, 195, 198, 201, 274–275, 280, 283, 282–287, 366–368, 377–378, 379–385, 387 **Net-text:** Descriptive Writing, Expository Writing, Persuasive Writing, Responding to Literature, Report Writing

College and Career Readiness Standard 3. Write narratives to develop real or imagined experiences or events using effective technique, well-chosen details, and well-structured event sequences.

Text Types and Purposes (continued)

Grade 2 Standard 3. Write narratives in which they recount a well-elaborated event or short sequence of events, include details to describe actions, thoughts, and feelings, use temporal words to signal event order, and provide a sense of closure.

Student Edition pages: 1, 15, 50, 52, 53, 55, 56, 57, 59, 60, 63, 64–69, 72–73, 82–83, 84–85, 104, 105, 110, 225, 357, 377–378, 395, 454

Net-text: Narrative Writing, Expository Writing, Creative Writing

Production and Distribution of Writing

College and Career Readiness Standard 4. Produce clear and coherent writing in which the development, organization, and style are appropriate to task, purpose, and audience.

Standard 4. (Begins in grade 3)

College and Career Readiness Standard 5. Develop and strengthen writing as needed by planning, revising, editing, rewriting, or trying a new approach.

Grade 2 Standard 5. With guidance and support from adults and peers, focus on a topic and strengthen writing as needed by revising and editing.

Student Edition pages: 5, 10–11, 21, 26, 44–45, 57, 70–77, 95, 108–115, 134–135, 144–150, 151, 170–171, 180–181, 190–191, 198, 204, 222–223, 238–239, 248–249, 288–291, 302, 372–375, 377

Interactive Whiteboard Lessons: Descriptive Writing, Narrative Writing, Expository Writing, Persuasive Writing, Responding to Literature, Creative Writing, Report Writing

Net-text: Descriptive Writing, Narrative Writing, Expository Writing, Persuasive Writing, Responding to Literature, Creative Writing, Report Writing

College and Career Readiness Standard 6. Use technology, including the Internet, to produce and publish writing and to interact and collaborate with others.

Grade 2 Standard 6. With guidance and support from adults, use a variety of digital tools to produce and publish writing, including in collaboration with peers.

Student Edition pages: 16–19, 33, 35, 36–37, 292, 295–297

Interactive Whiteboard Lessons: Descriptive Writing, Narrative Writing, Expository Writing, Persuasive Writing, Response to Literature, Creative Writing, Research Writing

Net-text: Report Writing

Research to Build and Present Knowledge

College and Career Readiness Standard 7. Conduct short as well as more sustained research projects based on focused questions, demonstrating understanding of the subject under investigation.

Grade 2 Standard 7. Participate in shared research and writing projects (e.g., read a number of books on a single topic to produce a report; record science observations).	**Student Edition pages:** 16–19, 42, 46–47, 120–121, 158–159, 256–272, 276–277, 278–279, 282–291, 293, 309 **Net-text:** Descriptive Writing, Report Writing

College and Career Readiness Standard 8. Gather relevant information from multiple print and digital sources, assess the credibility and accuracy of each source, and integrate the information while avoiding plagiarism.

Grade 2 Standard 8. Recall information from experiences or gather information from provided sources to answer a question.	**Student Edition pages:** 29, 50, 53–55, 59, 61–63, 83, 84–85, 86–87, 258, 271, 273–275, 277–279, 280–289, 370, 389 **Net-text:** Narrative Writing, Report Writing

College and Career Readiness Standard 9. Draw evidence from literary or informational texts to support analysis, reflection, and research.

Standard 9. (Begins in grade 4)

Range of Writing

College and Career Readiness Standard 10. Write routinely over extended time frames (time for research, reflection, and revision) and shorter time frames (a single sitting or a day or two) for a range of tasks, purposes, and audiences.

Standard 10. (Begins in grade 3)

Language Standards

Conventions of Standard English

College and Career Readiness Standard 1. Demonstrate command of the conventions of standard English grammar and usage when writing or speaking.

Grade 2 Standard 1. Demonstrate command of the conventions of standard English grammar and usage when writing or speaking.

a. Use collective nouns (e.g., *group*).	**File Cabinet:** Understanding Collective Nouns

Conventions of Standard English (continued)

b. Form and use frequently occurring irregular plural nouns (e.g., *feet, children, teeth, mice, fish*).	**Student Edition pages: 424–425**
c. Use reflexive pronouns (e.g., *myself, ourselves*).	**File Cabinet:** Reflexive Pronouns
d. Form and use the past tense of frequently occurring irregular verbs (e.g., *sat, hid, told*).	**Student Edition pages: 468** **GrammarSnap:** Irregular Verbs
e. Use adjectives and adverbs, and choose between them depending on what is to be modified.	**Student Edition pages: 349–349, 350–351** **GrammarSnap:** Adjectives, Adjectives to Compare, Adverbs
f. Produce, expand, and rearrange complete simple and compound sentences (e.g., *The boy watched the movie; The little boy watched the movie; The action movie was watched by the little boy*).	**GrammarSnap:** Complete Sentences

College and Career Readiness Standard 2. Demonstrate command of the conventions of standard English capitalization, punctuation, and spelling when writing.

Grade 2 Standard 2. Demonstrate command of the conventions of standard English capitalization, punctuation, and spelling when writing.

a. Capitalize holidays, product names, and geographic names.	**Student Edition pages: 328, 418–419** **GrammarSnap:** Capitalization of Days, Months, Holidays; Capitalization of Proper Nouns
b. Use commas in greetings and closings of letters.	**Student Edition pages: 150–151, 408–409** **Net-text:** Persuasive Writing
c. Use an apostrophe to form contractions and frequently occurring possessives.	**Student Edition pages: 332, 339, 410–413** **GrammarSnap:** Contractions, Apostrophes to Show Possession
d. Generalize learned spelling patterns when writing words (e.g., cage → badge; boy → boil).	**Student Edition pages: 429–438**
e. Consult reference materials, including beginning dictionaries, as needed to check and correct spellings.	**Student Edition pages: 256, 268–269, 389, 429** **Net-text:** Report Writing

Knowledge of Language

College and Career Readiness Standard 3. Apply knowledge of language to understand how language functions in different contexts, to make effective choices for meaning or style, and to comprehend more fully when reading or listening.

Grade 2 Standard 3. Use knowledge of language and its conventions when writing, speaking, reading, or listening.

a. Compare formal and informal uses of English.

Student Edition pages: 2, 12, 38, 50, 57, 126, 150, 164, 171, 208, 256, 290, 298, 324, 370, 400

Net-text: Descriptive Writing, Persuasive Writing, Creative Writing, Report Writing

Getting-Started Activities

The *Write Source* Student Edition is full of helpful resources that students can access throughout the year while they are developing their writing skills.

Getting-started activities are provided as copy masters on TE pages 580–582. (See the answer keys on TE page 583.) These activities will

- help students discover the kinds of information available in different sections of the book
- teach students how to access that information
- familiarize students with the layout of the book

The more familiar students are with the text, the more proficient they will be in using it as a resource.

Scavenger Hunts

Students enjoy using scavenger hunts to become familiar with a book. The scavenger hunts we provide can be done in small groups or as a class. They are designed for oral answers, but you may want to photocopy the pages for students to write on. You may also vary the procedure by first having students take turns finding the items and then, on the next scavenger hunt, challenging students to "race" for the answers.

After your students have completed each scavenger hunt, you can challenge them to create their own versions. For example, small groups can work together to create "Find the Fours" scavenger hunts and then exchange their "hunts" with other groups.

Special Challenge: Develop questions that teams of students try to answer, using the book. Pattern this activity after a popular game show.

Other Activities

- **All-School Reference** Have students write down all the subject areas they study and list under each heading the parts of the *Write Source* text that might help them in that subject.
- **Pen Pal Letter** Have students imagine that they are each going to send a copy of *Write Source* to a pen pal in another state or country. Ask students to write a letters telling their pen pals about the book.
- **Favorite Feature** Give your students the following assignment: Find one page, one short section, one set of guidelines, one illustration, one writing sample, or one chart you think is interesting, entertaining, stimulating, valuable, and so on. Students should prepare to share their discoveries with members of their discussion group or with the entire class.
- **5 W's and H** Have students develop *Who? What? When? Where? Why?* and *How?* questions from *Write Source*—for example, *What is step one in the writing process?* Students should then exchange questions with a partner and search for answers in the textbook. Afterward, partners may discuss each other's answers. (This activity can also be used as a search contest.)

This page is intentionally left blank

HOUGHTON MIFFLIN HARCOURT

WRITE SOURCE

Authors
Dave Kemper, Patrick Sebranek, and Verne Meyer

Illustrator
Chris Krenzke

GREAT SOURCE.

HOUGHTON MIFFLIN HARCOURT

Welcome to the Teacher's Edition!

Every child needs to learn about the world—and the world needs to learn about every child. Writing is the key to achieving both goals. With the *Write Source* program, your students will learn about the world as they learn to write, and they'll discover their unique voices in the process.

The Student Edition will guide your students on a journey. Along the way, your students will hear the voices of other writers speaking to them from the many accessible models.

The Teacher's Edition will guide you on this journey as well. In the following pages, you'll find not only lesson objectives and instructions, but also these special features at point of use:
■ Teaching Tips
■ Grammar Connections
■ Literature Connections
■ Writer's Craft Connections
■ Technology Connections
■ Notes for English Language Learners
■ Accommodations for Struggling Learners
■ Enrichments for Advanced Learners

Welcome to the journey! Welcome to *Write Source*.

Thanks to the Teachers!

This program would not have been possible without the input of many teachers and administrators from across the nation. As we originally developed this K–12 series, we surveyed hundreds of teaching professionals, and as we revised this series, we have implemented the feedback of even more. Our grateful thanks go out to each of you. We couldn't have done it without you!

ii

Reviewers

Genevieve Bodnar NBCT
Youngstown City Schools
Youngstown, Ohio

Mary M. Fischer
Arlington Public Schools
Arlington, Massachusetts

Cynthia Fontenot
Green T. Lindon Elementary
Lafayette, Louisiana

Heather Hagstrum
Unified School District #475
Ft. Riley, Kansas

Lisa Kickbusch
Pattonville School District
St. Ann, Missouri

Michele A. Lewis
Pattonville School District
St. Ann, Missouri

Joyce Martin
Forest Ridge
    Elementary School
Howard County
Laurel, Maryland

Kim T. Mickle
Alief Independent
    School District
Houston, Texas

Lisa D. Miller
Greater Clark County Schools
Jeffersonville, Indiana

Karen A. Reid
Rosemead School District
Rosemead, California

Roslyn Rowley-Penk
Renton School District
Renton, Washington

Jeannine M. Shirley, M. Ed.
White Hall School District
White Hall, Arkansas

Tanya Smith
Frankford Elementary School
Frankford, Delaware

Quick Guide

The *Write Source* Voice

For more than 30 years, our student books have spoken directly to students. We see ourselves as writers speaking to other writers.

As a result, the *Write Source* voice is always encouraging, like an older classmate who genuinely wants a younger one to succeed. We believe that every student can learn to write and that every writer can improve. Throughout this book, your students will hear a voice that says, "You can do it!"

In the same way, the material in the wraparound text speaks directly to you. After all, we are teachers speaking to other teachers, and so we use the same encouraging voice.

Whether you're a seasoned writing teacher or a fresh new face, we are certain that these materials in your hands can make a big difference for your students. We hope you agree!

The Process of Writing

The first section of the book provides an introduction to the writing process.

The chapter "One Writer's Process" lets students see how another second-grade writer works through the process of prewriting, writing, revising, editing, and publishing.

Integrating the Six Traits

Write Source fully integrates the six traits of writing into the writing process. Prewriting focuses on ideas and organization. Writing adds a focus on voice. Revising focuses on the first three traits and also word choice and sentence fluency. Editing zeroes in on conventions, while publishing features the added trait of presentation.

Contents

The Process of Writing

Wraparound Feature

Teaching Tip

Throughout the wraparound, you'll find special strategies for making the lesson come alive for your students.

Contents   **v**

The Forms of Writing

Descriptive Writing

Creating the Forms of Writing

The writing units in *Write Source* focus on creating the fundamental forms of writing:

- Descriptive
- Narrative
- Expository
- Persuasive
- Response to Literature
- Creative
- Research

Each writing assignment includes instruction, examples, and activities that lead students through the writing process. The material works well for whole-class instruction, writing workshop minilessons, and self-paced individual work time.

Writing Across the Curriculum

Special assignments after each of the major forms help your students write in their content areas: social studies, math, science, and practical writing. Whether you teach these subjects or partner with team teachers, these content-area assignments can help your students succeed throughout their day.

Wraparound Features

Materials

At the beginning of each unit, consult this box to find out what materials you need to have on hand to teach the lesson.

Copy Masters

These features tell you what classroom presentation aides exist to help you deliver the lesson.

Benchmark Papers

Check this feature to find out what benchmark papers you can use to show your students a range of performance.

Teaching the Core Units

Each unit begins with an accessible model with response questions, helping students make the reading-writing connection.

Afterward, the text leads students step-by-step through the process of creating a similar piece of writing. Concrete activities help students do the following:

- select a topic
- gather details
- organize details
- write a strong beginning
- build a solid middle
- create an effective ending
- revise for ideas, organization, voice, word choice, or sentence fluency
- edit for conventions
- publish work with polished presentation
- assess writing using traits-based rubrics

Wraparound Feature

Grammar Connection

Each unit overview suggests grammar activities to cover in the unit. Grammar Connection boxes then help you pinpoint the places to integrate instruction.

Contents   **vii**

Expository Writing

Writing Workshop

If you use the writing workshop approach, note how each activity in the core writing units can function as a minilesson. You can use these minilesson activities . . .

■ to direct the whole class before individual writing time,

■ to instruct a group of writers who are ready to learn a new skill, or

■ to provide scaffolding for an individual writer who gets stuck.

Throughout the wraparound, you'll find other helpful hints for applying the material in a writing workshop.

Wraparound Feature

Writer's Craft

These features help you inspire students to write the way professional writers do so. They feature techniques used by the great writers as well as interesting anecdotes and quotations.

Differentiating Instruction

Each of the core units provides three levels of form-specific assignments:

1. **Paragraph:** Students who are struggling—or who need an introduction to the form—can create a strong paragraph in the appropriate form.

2. **Essay:** Middle-level students can create, revise, and edit a multiparagraph essay in the form.

3. **Special Forms:** Advanced students can work on more challenging forms that connect to science, math, social studies, or practical writing.

Also, because the *Write Source* series follows a consistent format throughout its K–12 line, students who need further differentiation can work at a grade below (or above) their classmates.

Wraparound Features

English Language Learners
These boxes provide differentiation tips to help English language learners.

Struggling Learners
Consult this feature to adjust the lesson for those who are struggling.

Advanced Learners
These boxes feature tips for challenging students who excel.

Contents   ix

Responding to Literature

Connecting to Literature

Write Source is designed to work with your existing reading program by providing writing-based opportunities for students to explore reading.

- Writing a response paragraph
- Reviewing a fiction book
- Reviewing a nonfiction book
- Comparing two fiction books
- Responding to a poem
- Responding to literature in assessments

The text also teaches students to write three literary forms: stories, plays, and poems. By learning the basic vocabulary of prose, playwriting, and poetry through writing, your students will be better ready to read these forms.

Wraparound Feature

 Literature Connections

These features help you use age-appropriate literary works to teach students special writing techniques. You'll find interesting insights into the works and lives of favorite writers as well as fresh ways to use literature to teach writing.

Tapping Creativity

The *Write Source* series promotes creativity even in academic writing assignments. However, this section allows you and your students to develop forms that are especially inventive:

- Add-On Story
- Play
- Rhyming Poem
- Name Poem
- ABC Poem
- Tongue Twister
- Shape Poem
- Terse Verse
- Diamond Poem
- 5 W's Poem

Research shows a direct connection between enjoyment and learning. Think how quickly a student masters a favorite video game or learns all the words to a favorite song. By letting students write for the joy of it, you can awaken in them a lifelong love of writing.

Creative Writing

Contents   **xi**

Writing Reports

The step-by-step instructions in the "Report Writing" section help students learn to do the following:
- use the library
- use the Internet
- understand books and periodicals
- find sources
- interview sources
- create a report
- create a multimedia presentation

Equipping Students to Learn

This section focuses on the skills of speaking and listening, writing to learn, and conducting oneself in a classroom. These skills are crucial to success in all classes.

Wraparound Feature

 Technology Connections

In these features, you'll see connections to *Write Source Online* www.hmheducation.com/writesource. *Write Source Online* includes Interactive Whiteboard Lessons, Net-text, Bookshelf, GrammarSnap, Portfolio, and the File Cabinet.

Basic Grammar and Writing

The blue pages help your students practice working with the basic building blocks of language:

- "Working with Words" introduces five of the parts of speech and models how they are used in a sentence.
- "Building Sentences" helps students understand the parts of a sentence, create complete sentences, fix sentence problems, and combine sentences for greater flow.
- "Writing Paragraphs" models the topic sentence, supporting sentences, and closing sentence of paragraphs and helps reinforce paragraph indenting.

With clear rules, simple explanations, engaging examples, and fun activities, this section provides short minilessons to help students understand and apply the fundamentals of grammar and writing.

xii

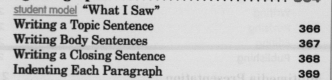

Basic Grammar and Writing

Contents **xiii**

A Writer's Resource

Creating Resourceful Writers

This section equips students with specific, traits-based strategies that they will use again and again during the writing process. Each new concept is introduced by a question that many of your students have asked at one time or another—followed by an answer to the question and a specific strategy for implementing the answer.

Teaching Conventions

The "Proofreader's Guide" provides a handy reference to the basic rules of English, along with activities to practice the rules.

As you work through the writing units earlier in the book, you will find cross-references to the "Proofreader's Guide" and "Basic Grammar and Writing." You'll also find cross-references to the grammar activities in the *SkillsBook* and *Write Source Online* GrammarSnap. Integrated grammar instruction allows students to use the rules in context and understand not just the "what" of grammar, but also the "why."

You can use all the grammar that is suggested—or you can target the grammar to your students' specific needs. The choice is yours.

Proofreader's Guide

1

Why Write?

The main reason to write is to communicate with others. Writing is an important way to share your feelings, thoughts, stories, and ideas.

Writing will help you . . .

- **Share with others.** You can tell your friends and family all about you in letters, cards, notes, and e-mail messages.

- **Remember more.** You can remember better when you write facts and ideas in your own words.

- **Learn more about you.** You will discover your own thoughts and feelings by writing.

- **Have fun.** You can imagine wonderful things in the stories, poems, and plays you write.

Remember: The more you read, the better your writing will be.

Why Write?

As you introduce students to the writing process, keep in mind that many students at this stage in their writing experience will be as concerned with forming letters as they are with forming ideas. Students will become more comfortable exploring ideas and feelings through writing once they feel that they have mastered the physical act of writing.

With this in mind, offer praise and encouragement whenever students attempt to write. Focus on the best parts of a student's writing, whether that is the formation of the letters or the development of ideas. The goal is to instill a sense of pride so that students will be eager to write.

Have students share pieces of writing they have done, including letters, poems, and stories. Have them identify the purpose of their writing. Did they write to have fun? Did they write to remember something? Did they write to tell a friend about an interesting experience?

The Writing Process Overview

Common Core Standards Focus

Writing 5: With guidance and support from adults and peers, focus on a topic and strengthen writing as needed by revising and editing.

Language 1: Demonstrate command of the conventions of standard English grammar and usage when writing or speaking.

Language 2: Demonstrate command of the conventions of standard English capitalization, punctuation, and spelling when writing.

Writing Process

- **Prewriting** Select a topic, gather details, and talk with a partner about ideas.
- **Writing** Write a topic sentence, add details in body sentences, and write a closing sentence.
- **Revising** Improve writing by reading it aloud, looking for the traits, and changing words to make the writing clear.
- **Editing** Check capitalization, punctuation, and spelling.
- **Publishing** Make a neat final copy and share it with others.

Focus on the Traits

- **Ideas** Thinking of a good topic and listing details about it
- **Organization** Making sure the beginning names the topic, the middle adds details, and the ending shares a final thought
- **Voice** Using a natural-sounding voice, as if talking to a friend
- **Word Choice** Using words that make the writing clear
- **Sentence Fluency** Writing different lengths of sentences
- **Conventions** Checking for errors in capitalization, punctuation, and spelling

 Technology Connections

Write Source Online
www.hmheducation.com/writesource

- **Net-text**
- **Bookshelf**
- **GrammarSnap**
- **Portfolio**
- **Writing Network features**
- **File Cabinet**

Interactive Whiteboard Lessons

Suggested Writing Process Unit (Four Weeks)

Day	Writing and Skills Instruction	Student Edition		SkillsBook	Daily Language Workouts
		Writing Process Unit	Resource Units*		
WEEK 1 1–5	Getting-Started Activities, TE pages TE-61 and 580–583 **Why Write?**	1			4–5, 79
WEEK 2 6–10	**Using the Writing Process** **Writing in Journals and Learning Logs**	4–5 306–309	439–446 (+)	95–96	6–7, 80
11–12	**One Writer's Process** (Model, Prewriting, Writing)	6–9	401–414 (+)	41–42	8–9, 81
WEEK 3 13–15	**One Writer's Process** (Revising, Editing, Publishing)	10–15	417–426 (+)	83–84	
	Working with a Partner	16–19			
	Learning to Listen	316–317			
16–18	**Understanding the Writing Traits** (Ideas)	20–21			10–11, 82
	(Organization, Voice)	22–23			
WEEK 4	(Word Choice, Sentence Fluency, Conventions)	24–25	449–454 (+)	113–114	
	Connecting the Process and the Traits	26–27			
19–20	**Using a Rubric**	28–31	457–476 (+)	164–165	
	Publishing and Portfolios	32–37			

* These units are also located in the back of the *Teacher's Edition*. Resource Units include "Basic Grammar and Writing," "A Writer's Resource," and "Proofreader's Guide."
(+) This activity is located in a different section of the *Write Source Student Edition*. If students have already completed this activity, you may wish to review it at this time.

Teacher's Notes for the Writing Process

This overview for the writing process includes some specific teaching suggestions for the unit.

Writing Focus

Using the Writing Process (pages 4–5)

Young writers can gradually learn about the stages of the writing process, a series of choices a writer makes as she or he shares ideas. Prewriting involves different ways of planning. A first draft is a writer's first try at getting ideas down on paper. Revising means making changes to parts of the writing that don't work. Proofreading means checking for spelling, capital letters, and punctuation.

Working with a Partner (pages 16–19)

Demonstrate revising with a partner by conducting the following activity with a confident student. Ask the student to read one of his or her short first drafts. (Put the draft on an overhead or a chart so that all the students can see it.) Mention parts you like, and ask questions about parts that are weak. Ask the student to suggest ways to improve the writing. If possible, reverse roles and let the student react to the strengths and weaknesses of a short note or paragraph you have written.

Writing Traits (pages 20–27)

The traits of good writing are present in the books that children love to hear over and over again. Books by William Steig, Cynthia Rylant, Mem Fox, Arnold Lobel, and Tomie dePaola are among the favorites of many young readers and listeners. Check them yourself for the traits of good writing. You will find interesting ideas, good organization, personal voice, well-chosen words, and more! The traits of good writing give students and teachers "handles" for speaking about written work. When students are learning to evaluate their own writing, they need something specific to look for.

Rubric (pages 28–31)

A rubric is simply a list of criteria by which a piece of writing may be assessed. It should include a list of traits or qualities found in an effective piece of writing. Students should always know beforehand what criteria will be used to assess their work.

Academic Vocabulary

Read aloud the academic terms, as well as the descriptions and questions. Model for students how to read one question and answer it. Have partners monitor their understanding and seek clarification of the terms by working through the meanings and questions together.

The Writing Process

Writing Focus
- Using the Writing Process
- Working with a Partner
- Writing Traits
- Rubric
- Publishing and Portfolios

Academic Vocabulary

Work with a partner. Read the meanings and share your answers.
1. A draft is a piece of writing that you have not finished yet.
   Why might you write a draft first?
2. A process is an order of steps.
   Tell the process of making a sandwich.
3. To create something means to make it.
   What can you create out of paper, scissors, and glue?

Publishing and Portfolios (pages 32–37)

Half the fun of a creative endeavor is sharing it with others. And that's exactly what publishing is all about—preparing writing to be shared with others. It is the natural culmination of the writing process. Of course, not every piece of writing gets published.

Brainstorm with children some different ways books and writing can be illustrated. For example, besides drawing, students could choose rubbings, painting, collage, photos, cartoon art, or cutouts from magazines and catalogs. (Offering a variety of media for illustration can involve more students in this enjoyable process.)

Compiling portfolios helps students see over a year's time how their writing has changed and improved. At the same time, a portfolio lets them see what part of their writing needs to be improved.

3

Writers do their work in many different ways. Tim slowly builds his stories, thinking carefully about each new idea. Gina finds it helpful to draw pictures as she writes. José likes to talk about his writing as he goes along. There are many ways to get ready to write.

In this part of the book, you will learn all about writing from using the writing process to publishing your writing.

The Writing Process

On the board, write headings for the three ways to get ready to write mentioned in the first paragraph:

- Think Quietly
- Draw Pictures
- Talk About Ideas

Read each heading aloud. Ask students to raise their hand if that's what they do or would like to do to get ready to write. Record under the heading the number of students who raise their hand.

Point out that not everyone chose the same way to get ready to write. Explain that there is no right way. A student may also use several of these ways to prepare to write.

Have students discuss why they might choose each way and how each way can help them get ready to write.

- Some people don't like to talk about their ideas until they've had time to think about them. Thinking quietly helps them plan their writing.
- Some people like to draw. Drawing pictures helps them see what they want to write about.
- Some people think better when they talk out loud. When you tell someone your ideas, they might have some other ideas for you.

Family Connection Letters

As you begin this unit, send home the Writing Process Family Connection letter, which describes what students will be learning.

- Letter in English (TE p. 562)
- Letter in Spanish (TE p. 570)

Using the Writing Process

Objectives
- establish good writing habits
- understand the five steps in the writing process

Beginning writers are likely to think of each step as separate from the others. Explain that the steps depend on each other and that, sometimes, writers may go back to an earlier step.

Prewriting

Emphasize that the first thing students need to do before they can begin to write is to choose a topic.

Writing

Explain to students that during the writing step they put their ideas and details from the prewriting step into **paragraph form**.

Revising

Continue to reinforce the connections among the different steps of the writing process. Point out to students that in this step they read and improve what they wrote in the second step.

4

Using the Writing Process

Do you have stories to tell, reports to give, letters to send, invitations to write, and ideas to share? Well then, join us in learning about the writing process and see what you can create.

Talk it over.

1. What is your favorite piece of writing?
2. How did you write it?

Prewriting ▶ Planning Your Writing

When you prewrite, you **choose** your topic and **gather** details about it.

Writing ▶ Writing the First Draft

When you write a first draft, you **identify** your topic and **add** supporting details.

Revising ▶ Improving Your Writing

When you revise, you **change** parts to make your writing better. **Use** the traits of writing as a guide.

Editing ▶ Checking for Conventions

When you edit, you **check** for spelling, punctuation, and capitalization errors. Then you **correct** any that you find.

Publishing ▶ Sharing Your Final Copy

When you publish your writing, you **make** a neat, final copy and **share** it with others.

Editing

Suggest to students that when they edit their writing they use a colored pencil. By doing so, they will be less likely to miss any of their corrections when they make their final copy.

Have students start a personal list of words they frequently misspell. They can refer to this list during the editing step.

Publishing

Provide time for students to look at and discuss the ideas for publishing on SE page 33.

The pencil icon appears throughout the book at each step in the writing process. Have students skim SE pages 66 through 69 of the Narrative Writing unit and identify the pencil icon used to signal each step in the writing assignment.

Lead a class discussion for the **Talk it over** activity. Ask students to recall favorite writing assignments or projects from previous years.

Discuss the basics of keeping a **writing journal** *(see below)*. To encourage daily journal writing, set aside 5 to 10 minutes of class time at the beginning of each day.

✽ For more about keeping a writing journal and a writer's notebook, see SE pages 372–375.

Teaching Tip: Keeping a Writing Journal

Help students set up their writing journals and provide a few tips to get them started.

Students can use any kind of notebook with lined pages for their writing journal. They can also use a three-ring binder with loose-leaf paper. This format enables students to write about an idea and then add a drawing or more details to that idea later by just adding blank pages.

Students can also keep a journal on a computer.

Tell students to write the date at the top of each day's entry and then to write for 5 to 10 minutes. These questions can help them find things to write about.

● What have I seen or heard lately that I thought was funny or interesting?

● What special person, event, or place do I want to remember?
● What ideas have I had that keep popping up in my mind?

At first students may have trouble writing for five to ten minutes, but this should get easier as they practice regular journal writing.

One Writer's Process

6

Objective

- evaluate one writer's step-by-step progress through the writing process

Throughout this book, students will encounter writing samples to use as models for their own writing. At first, they may follow the samples very closely, perhaps even mimicking the sentence patterns and organization of ideas. Later, as they begin to feel more comfortable and confident as writers, they can see each sample more as an example of how another writer approached the assignment.

Writer's Craft

Different processes: Every writer follows a different process. Encourage students to discover their own version of the writing process. Tell them the following:

"Some professional writers are gardeners. They plant ideas like seeds and water them and tend them to see what grows.

"Other professional writers are builders. They stack ideas like bricks and follow very specific plans to make something wonderful.

"What kind of writer are you?"

One Writer's Process

Monica's class had fun learning about holidays from around the world. Monica's teacher asked each student to write a paragraph about one of the holidays.

Follow along to see how Monica used the steps in the writing process to complete her paragraph.

Materials

Blank overhead transparency (TE p. 11)

Chart paper (TE p. 13)

Prewriting ▶ Planning Your Writing

When you prewrite, you choose your topic and gather details about it. You can use drawings during prewriting.

Choose	Monica decided to write about a special holiday in Japan, Children's Day.
Study	Monica remembered what she had learned about her topic in class. She also read about her topic.
Draw	Monica drew pictures of the details she wanted to write about.

Monica's Pictures

English Language Learners

Explain that *pre-* is a word part that means "before" and that *prewriting* means "before writing." Provide additional examples, such as *preview*, *pretest*, and *prewash*, and discuss the meaning of each word.

Teaching Tip: Details

The story of the blind men and the elephant involves five people who each experience a different part of the animal. Each comes away thinking an elephant is—like a tree (leg), like a rope (tail), like a huge snake (trunk), like a piece of canvas (ear), and like a wall (side). Discuss why many details are important.

Prewriting Planning Your Writing

Explain to students that the topic is what a piece of writing is about. Writers choose topics that they

- know something about,
- want to learn more about, and
- enjoy writing about.

Discuss what it means to gather details. Select a simple classroom object such as a pencil sharpener. Ask students to give you details to describe it. How big is it? What color is it? What does it feel like? What does it smell like? What sound does it make? Where is it located? What is it used for? You could read or tell the story of the blind men and the elephant to illustrate the importance of gathering lots of details. See Teaching Tip below.

Ask students where else they might find details about the Japanese holiday Children's Day. Students may suggest the following ideas:

- Search on the Internet.
- Look in an encyclopedia.
- Ask a Japanese friend or neighbor.

Make sure students understand that details are not right or wrong. However, when they are gathering details, they can ask themselves questions such as the following to decide if they should include a specific detail:

- Is this detail something that I find interesting?
- Will my readers understand the topic better if I include this detail?

Writing **Writing the First Draft**

Point out that the first draft is the writer's chance to put all the prewriting ideas and details into sentences on paper. It's called a "first draft" because the writer will make changes and improvements before writing the final copy.

8

Writing ▶ Writing the First Draft

When you write your first draft, you put your ideas in sentence form.

These are the things Monica did to write her first draft.

Look Before she started writing, Monica looked at her drawings about Children's Day.

State In her first sentence, Monica told what she would write about.

Add Monica's next sentences added ideas and details about her topic.

Most of the details in my paragraph come from my pictures.

Paper hats

Monica's First Draft

Monica's First Draft

> I lerned about Children's Day in school. It is a special day for the kids in Japan. They do fun stuff on this day. It comes on May 5. Children do not go to school on Children's Day they fly colorful fish kites from tall poles. They where paper hats and eat rice cakes. i think the fish kites would be fun to see. I wonder if rice cakes taste good.

Talk it over.

Which details from her pictures (page 7) did Monica include in her first draft?

Advanced Learners

As an extension to the **Talk it over** activity, challenge students to work together to create their own Children's Day tradition. Encourage them to draw pictures of the details and then write a paragraph explaining the new tradition.

Some students may not be able to refrain from pointing out the convention mistakes in the paragraph. Acknowledge the errors and explain that when you draft a piece of writing, you want to focus on ideas and organization, not on spelling and punctuation. Those can be checked later during the editing process. Tell students that they will see that Monica corrects any mistakes later when she edits her paragraph.

Ask students why they think Monica included the last two sentences in the paragraph. Help students understand that these closing sentences

- show Monica's interest and feelings about the topic and
- give readers something to think about after they finish reading.

Tell students that they can try to do the same things when they write their ending for a piece of writing.

Talk it over.

Answers

Monica uses the following details from her pictures:

- fish kites
- paper hats
- rice cakes
- children having a day off from school

Revising Improving Your Writing

One way to help students understand revising and editing is to talk about big changes and small changes.

Big changes (revising) include the following:
- crossing out a word, phrase, or sentence;
- adding a better word, phrase, or sentence;
- changing words to make the writing clearer; and
- moving words or sentences.

Point out that once all the big changes of revising are done, it is easier to look for and correct the small changes. Small changes (editing) include the following:
- adding a missing letter in a misspelled word,
- adding a period to the end of a sentence, or
- making a lowercase letter into a capital letter.

10

Revising ▶ Improving Your Writing

When you revise, you try to improve your writing. You should change any parts that are unclear or hard to follow.

This is what Monica did to revise her paragraph.

Review Monica read her first draft to herself.

Share Next, Monica shared her first draft with a classmate.

Improve Then she changed parts to improve her writing.

I moved one idea and replaced another one. I also added a new detail.

Monica's Revising

One Writer's Process **11**

I lerned about Children's Day in

school. It is a special day for the kids

Children have fun
in Japan. ~~They do fun stuff~~ on this day.

It comes on May 5. Children do not

go to school on Children's Day they fly

colorful fish kites from tall poles. They

wrapped in leaves
where paper hats and eat rice cakes. i

think the fish kites would be fun to see. I

wonder if rice cakes taste good.

Talk it over.

What changes did Monica make?

Struggling Learners

To ensure that students understand the changes Monica made to her paragraph, read aloud the paragraph with the changes. You may want to have a volunteer read an overhead of the corrected paragraph complete with the mistakes in conventions. You can then use the paragraph on the overhead to show the convention corrections, which students will learn about on SE page 12.

Monica's Revising

Notice that Monica left space between lines so she had room to make changes. Students will benefit from a brief discussion of the proofreading marks used on this page before discussing the revision.

Talk it over.

You may want to point out the proofreading marks on the inside back cover of the text. Discuss and explain the reasoning behind each revision.

- (An idea is cut.) The phrase, "They do fun stuff" is cut because it is too general. It doesn't create a clear picture or idea.
- (An idea is added.) Changing the sentence to "Children have fun on this day" adds an idea that's important for the reader to know. The sentences that follow are all about the ways that the children have fun, so this change also improves the flow of ideas.
- (An idea is moved.) Moving the sentence with the date is an improvement because now the date of the holiday comes right after the name of the holiday.
- (New details are added.) Adding the interesting detail about rice cakes wrapped in leaves is an improvement because this information helps readers know more about the food the children eat on Children's Day.

Editing Checking for Conventions

Talk about the importance of editing and how this step affects readers. Tell students that editing is about making the small final changes.

Invite students to practice using the editing and proofreading marks on the inside back cover of their *Write Source* text. Hand out a *Daily Language Workouts* paragraph or use a student model from a previous year. Talk through the editing process, reviewing the paragraph for one type of error at a time. For example, check capitalization of each first word in sentences and then check for end punctuation for each sentence. Afterward, check for other capitalization issues and misspelled or wrong words.

12

Editing ▶ Checking for Conventions

When you edit, you check for correct spelling, punctuation, and capitalization.

This is what Monica did to edit her writing.

Read   Monica read her revised paragraph for conventions.

Correct   Monica corrected any capitalization, punctuation, and spelling mistakes she found.

Recheck   Monica checked her writing one last time for mistakes.

I used the editing marks listed inside the back cover of the book. I also added a title— Children's Day!

One Writer's Process **13**

Monica's Editing

> Children's Day
>
> ~~learned~~
> I (lerned) about Children's Day
>
> in school. It comes on May 5. It is
>
> a special day for the kids in Japan.
>
> Children have fun on this day. Children
>
> do not go to school on Children's Day⊙
>
> ≡ they fly colorful fish kites from tall
>
> wear
> poles. They ~~where~~ paper hats and eat
>
> rice cakes wrapped in leaves. i think the
>   ≡
> fish kites would be fun to see. I wonder
>
> if rice cakes taste good.

Talk it over.

Which convention errors did Monica correct?

Monica's Editing

Have students focus on the editing marks and changes that Monica made to her paragraph.

If you created an overhead transparency for the revised paragraph (Struggling Learners, TE page 11), ask students to look at it and identify any errors in punctuation, capitalization, or spelling they see in the paragraph. Then discuss the mistakes highlighted in the call-outs. Pay special attention to the misspelling of the word *where*. Point out that words that sound the same, such as *where* and *wear*, are often confused.

✷ For more about using the right word, see SE pages 439–445.

Talk it over.

Monica uses . . .
- A circle around a word for a spelling error.
- A circle around a period to add a period.
- Three lines under a letter for making a lowercase letter into a capital letter (first word in the sentence and the word *I*).
- A delete mark to cross out a wrong word.
- A caret to replace a word or add a new word.

English Language Learners

Point out the homophones, such as *wear* and *where* in "Children's Day." Write each word and its meaning on chart paper to begin a class homophone chart. You might include simple sketches as visual cues to help students differentiate the meanings. Add homophone pairs to the chart as needed. Possible suggestions: *it's* and *its*; *too, two,* and *to; our* and *hour; their, there,* and *they're.*

Publishing Sharing Your Writing

You may want to emphasize the formatting elements of a final copy at this point. Your school may have a standard for the students' placement of names on assignments. Point out that Monica leaves one line between her title and the beginning of her paragraph. Remind students to indent the first line of their paragraphs as Monica did.

It may be hard for young writers to leave even margins for their paragraphs on each side because it is difficult for them to judge whether they can complete a word before reaching the edge of the paper. Tell them that it is easier to read a paper if each word is complete at the end of each line. Have them notice that words are not split in their *Write Source* book. That makes it easier for them to read!

14

Publishing ▶ Sharing Your Writing

When you publish your writing, you make a final copy and share it with others.

Complete   Monica made a final copy of her paragraph. She skipped a line after her title and indented the first line of her paragraph. Monica included all of her changes and corrections.

Share   Then Monica shared her paragraph by reading it out loud to her classmates.

I decided to draw a fish kite on my final copy.

Monica's Paragraph

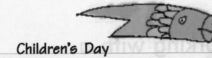

Children's Day

▶ (Skip)

▶ (Indent) I learned about Children's Day
in school. It comes on May 5. It is
a special day for the kids in Japan.
Children have fun on this day. Children
do not go to school on Children's Day.
They fly colorful fish kites from tall
poles. They wear paper hats and eat
rice cakes wrapped in leaves. I think
the fish kites would be fun to see. I
wonder if rice cakes taste good.

Talk it over.

1. What details in Monica's paragraph do
   you like the best? Name two.
2. What thoughts does Monica share in the
   last two sentences?

Monica's Paragraph

Have students explain in their own words why
Monica's writing is ready to share. This will
help you assess how well they have understood
the steps in the writing process. You may want
to ask the following questions:

- How did Monica's drawings help her add
  details to her writing?
- How did she put information in the best order
  (moved date)?
- Where did she add helpful details (rice cakes
  wrapped in leaves)?
- How did she correct capitalization (they, i),
  punctuation (period after Day), and spelling
  (learned)?
- Which word did she replace that was the
  wrong word (where, wear)?

Talk it over.

1. Answers will vary. Ask students to be very
   specific. For example, "I liked the part about
   rice cakes wrapped in leaves because I had
   rice wrapped in grape leaves, and it was
   delicious."
2. Monica shares her feelings. She would like
   to see fish kites. She wonders if she would
   like rice cakes.

Working with a
Partner

Objectives

- learn how to be a good partner by giving helpful responses
- understand the roles of the writer and the listener when working with a partner
- learn how to use a partner worksheet

Encourage students to write about topics that truly interest them and that reflect their own experiences. Try to allow time at the start of each day for students to share fun experiences they have had. Point out to students that their experiences are potential topics for their writing. Tell students to be sure to list these ideas in their writing journal.

Writing Workshop

Use this chapter to help create a writing community in your classroom. Emphasize that when students read and respond to each other's work, they must be respectful of one another while at the same time providing helpful comments and suggestions. Model this process by doing your own writing in front of the students and asking them for suggestions to revise your work.

16

Working with a
Partner

In art class, Luis made a coil pot, and he decided to write a story about it. He shared his story with a partner. She asked some questions and that gave Luis some good ideas to make his story even better.

Materials

Blank index cards (TE p. 17)

Helping One Another

Being a partner and having a partner is helpful as you go through the writing process.

Here are some ways partners can help one another during the writing process.

Talk Partners can talk about topics and details. Talking can help you **prewrite** and **write**.

Listen and Ask Partners can listen while a first draft is shared out loud. Partners ask questions to help **revise** the writing.

Check Partners can help check writing for conventions. Working together can help **edit** the writing.

Read Partners can read and enjoy a final copy. Reading is one way to **publish**.

Helping One Another

Students are probably familiar with having a partner on field trips and other group events, where pairs of students watch out for one another. Initiate students' work with partners by doing the following:

- Have students write their name on a blank index card. Collect the cards.
- At the start of each new writing assignment, mix the cards up and have volunteers select two cards at a time and read aloud each pair of names.

This section discusses student pairs who act as writing partners to help each other make their writing better.

Throughout the year, remind students that writing partners can be helpful during all the stages in the writing process. Encourage students to think and work collaboratively on all their writing projects.

English Language Learners

When assigning partners for the writing process, have students work with cooperative, considerate students who are proficient in English. It may be most effective if partnerships are ongoing throughout an entire unit so that students feel comfortable and confident sharing their work.

Copy Masters

Response Sheet (TE p. 19)

Being on a Team

Some students may be reluctant to work with a partner for various reasons, including shyness or lack of confidence. If you notice that partners are not able to share ideas, offer to become a temporary third member of their team. You can relieve students of some of the partner duties while encouraging them to apply the tips that are given for writers and listeners. After a while, most students should become comfortable enough to proceed without your participation.

When You Are the Writer

Encourage students to think about why they chose a topic. If they say "because I couldn't think of anything else" or "I don't know," their partner may think that they don't care about their topic.

Tell students to read clearly and slowly so that their partners do not miss any of their ideas.

When You Are the Listener

To make sure students know the difference between hurtful and helpful comments, conduct a **partner's workshop** (see below).

18

Being on a Team

Working with a partner is like being on a team. After writing a first draft, one team member reads his or her writing out loud. The other member listens and responds to the writing.

Partner Tips

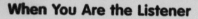

When You Are the Writer

Tell why you chose your topic.
Read your writing to your partner.
Pay attention to your partner's comments.

When You Are the Listener

Look at your partner.
Listen carefully to the writing.
Respond to the writing.
1. **Tell** your partner what you like.
2. **Ask** any questions you may have.

Teaching Tip: Partner's Workshop

Remind students that they are trying to help make their partner's writing better. They should not say things that will hurt their partner's feelings. The Response Sheet on SE page 19 is designed to prevent this from happening. You can use the following examples to illustrate how to offer constructive help:
- Helpful: Your idea about the game is good. I'd understand

it better if you explained all the rules.
- Hurtful: You don't seem to know anything about this game.

Point out that the helpful comment tells what the listener liked and then tells the writer what to do to make the writing even better. The hurtful comment doesn't offer any helpful advice.

Working with a Partner 19

Using a Response Sheet

You can also use a response sheet to review your partner's writing.

Laura's Response

Response Sheet

Writer: <u>Luis</u>   Listener: <u>Laura</u>

Title: <u>My Coil Pot</u>

1. One thing I like about your story:

   <u>I like the way you told about</u>

   <u>making the long snake of clay.</u>

2. One question I have about your story:

   <u>Who are you going to give the</u>

   <u>pot to?</u>

Using a Response Sheet

Review the sample Response Sheet and discuss how the responses might help the writer, Luis, improve his writing.

- The response to item 1 highlights a favorite part. Perhaps Luis will add more detail to this part to make it even more interesting.
- The response to item 2 is a question that Luis might want to answer in his story so other readers won't have the same question.

Photocopies of the reproducible Response Sheet (TE page 500) can be distributed whenever students work with a partner.

English Language Learners

When students begin to work with the Response Sheet, modify the activity by allowing them first to express their ideas orally. Have them dictate their thoughts to a classmate who can record them on paper.

Struggling Learners

Some students may have difficulty listening to a partner's story and jotting down notes simultaneously on their Response Sheet. Remind students that good notes can be words, phrases, or pictures. Tell them they can signal their partners to pause by using a gesture or a tap on the arm, so they can have time to jot down notes.

Understanding the Writing Traits

Understanding the Writing Traits

Objectives

- explore the six traits of effective writing
- apply the concepts of the traits to a piece of writing

The following three traits provide a focus during prewriting, drafting, and revising:

- Ideas
- Organization
- Voice

The remaining three traits relate more to the revising and editing processes:

- Word Choice
- Sentence Fluency
- Conventions

Explain to students that SE pages 20 through 25 cover the traits in detail and suggest ways of using them in writing.

20

Understanding the Writing Traits

You can use the **six traits of writing** listed below to help you do your best writing.

 Ideas — **Start with good ideas!**

 Organization — **Make your writing easy to follow.**

 Voice — **Sound like you are really interested in your topic.**

 Word Choice — **Choose your words carefully.**

 **Sentence Fluency** — **Use different lengths of sentences.**

 Conventions — **Follow the rules for writing.**

Materials

Oak tag strips (TE p. 22)

Blank index cards (TE p. 23)

English Language Learners

Help students conceptualize the word *trait* by pointing out that people have traits, or qualities, that make up how they look (hair and eye color) and how they behave (shy or funny). Explain that the six traits of writing work together to make a piece of writing fun and interesting to read.

Ideas

Start with good ideas!

Alita likes writing about her family. She thinks of good topics and gathers interesting details.

Topic **my baby sister**

Details **three months old**
cries when she is hungry
wears pink and yellow
smiles at me
sleeps a lot
looks like my baby pictures

practice

1. In a writing notebook, write down an interesting topic and at least three important details about it.
2. Share your ideas with a partner.

Copy Masters

Gathering Details (TE p. 21)

Word Choice (TE p. 24)

Sentence Fluency (TE p. 24)

Editing Checklist (TE p. 25)

Editing Practice (TE p. 25)

Ideas Start with good ideas!

Tell students that sometimes they can get a good idea for writing from their experiences. For example, on SE page 16, Luis made a coil pot and decided to write about that. Other times, students may choose as their topic something they simply like to write about. Alita chooses her baby sister as her topic because she likes writing about her family. Both Luis's and Alita's topics are good ideas because the writers find them interesting and fun to write about.

Explain that thinking of a good topic may take a little time. Point out to students that there are things they can do to help them think of a good topic for writing. For example, they can read stories and articles, flip through their writing journals, talk to friends and family members, and create lists.

✳ Have students refer to the Writing Ideas and Special Topics on SE pages 376–377 when they need help choosing topics.

Provide photocopies of the reproducible Gathering Details page (TE page 513). Circulate among students as they complete the **Practice.** Offer suggestions such as those on SE pages 376–377 if students are having trouble thinking of a topic or coming up with details.

Organization
Make your writing easy to follow.

Students probably have some idea of *beginning,* *middle,* and *ending* as these concepts relate to stories they have read. They now need to apply what they know about these concepts to writing. Before introducing students to this page, do this simple activity.

- Write the words *Beginning, Middle,* and *Ending* in large letters on separate oak tag strips.
- Arrange the words in the following order—*Middle, Ending,* and *Beginning*—on the chalkboard ledge or another place for students to see.
- Ask students to read aloud the words with you and to tell if the words are in the right order (no). Then ask students what it would be like to read a story in which the middle came first, the ending came next, and the beginning came last. (Students will probably say that the story would be silly and would not make sense.)
- Then have students help you put the words in order.
- Finally, ask students why it is important that their writing always have a beginning, a middle, and an ending in that order (so that the story, or report, is easy to read and makes sense).

22

Organization

Make your writing easy to follow.

Cole makes sure that his writing has a beginning, a middle, and an ending.

Our Sailing Adventure

> The **Beginning** names the topic.

Last summer, I had an adventure with my grandma. We went to the harbor in Baltimore to sail on a tall ship.

> The **Middle** adds details.

First, we pulled on ropes to help put up the sails. Then we sailed out to sea. Soon we couldn't even see land. Squawking seagulls flew around us. When the crew first fired a cannon, the noise and smoke scared me. Then I started laughing.

> The **Ending** shares my final thought.

Grandma and I had a great time. I can't wait for our next adventure.

Advanced Learners

Point out to students that organization is just as important within a paragraph as it is from paragraph to paragraph. Explain that writers often use words such as *first, next,* and *later* to help readers understand the order in which events happen. Have students read through Cole's second paragraph and identify words that make the organization of details clear *(First, Then, Soon, When, Then).* Have a volunteer read the paragraph without the signal words to demonstrate for students how important these words can be to understanding.

Voice

Sound like you are really interested in your topic.

Julian is really interested in his topic because he is writing about his dog. He likes to share ideas about him.

My Buddy

I'm Julian, and my dog is my best buddy. Can you guess what his name is? That's right! It's Buddy.

Buddy eats strange things. He chews on rugs and bones. He likes liver. Once he even ate a raw fish. He smelled awful after that.

Buddy always spends time with me. Every morning, he walks me to the school bus. He's always waiting at the bus stop when I get home. At night, my best buddy sleeps on my bed.

Write a story about an animal. Does your writing sound like you are really interested in your topic?

Voice Sound like you are really interested in your topic.

As students become more aware of formal language and develop a larger vocabulary, they may try to use the new vocabulary in their writing, often with mixed results. Instead of sounding natural, their writing voice may sometimes sound stilted and self-conscious.

Younger writers, however, generally tend to write with a natural voice that sounds very much like their speaking voice because they don't know any other way to sound. Take every opportunity available to praise students' natural writing voice and encourage them to continue to write this way.

The goal of the **Practice** activity is for students to recognize their natural voice. Young children, however, can get carried away when telling a story. To prevent students from rambling and to make sure they tell a story that has a beginning, a middle, and an ending, provide time for students to **plan their story** (see below).

Have students read their story to their partner. Partners can say if the written story sounds just like, sort of like, or not at all like the oral version.

Teaching Tip: Plan a Story

Not all students may have had pets or experiences with animals, but most will have read an animal story or have seen an animal in a movie or on a television program. Suggest that they retell one of these stories if they are having trouble coming up with an idea for a story.

- Distribute three blank index cards to each student. Tell students to write the word *Beginning* on one card, *Middle* on the next card, and *Ending* on the third card.
- Next, tell them to draw a picture or jot down a couple of words on each card to remind them of the

beginning, the middle, and the ending of their story.
- Students can use their index cards to tell their story to a partner, and then to help them write their story in the proper sequence.

Word Choice
Choose your words carefully.

After students read the sample sentences, ask these questions to help them understand the effect of clear, or specific, language.

- Which sentence is easier for you to picture in your mind? (the second sentence)
- Why is the second sentence easier to picture? (The word *tiptoed* shows exactly how Marcus came into the room. The word *kitchen* shows which room he came into.)
- Why do you think it is important for writers to use clear words like *tiptoed* and *kitchen*? (so readers can picture and understand what the writing is about)

To give students additional practice with choosing clear words, provide photocopies of the reproducible Word Choice page (TE page 514).

Sentence Fluency Use different lengths of sentences.

Read aloud the following sentences and then read aloud the sample sentences to help students appreciate the difference between short, choppy sentences and sentences of varied lengths:

Rover barked. He saw a rabbit. He chased it across the yard.

To give students additional practice with writing a variety of sentences, provide photocopies of the reproducible Sentence Fluency page (TE page 515).

24

Word Choice

Choose your words carefully.

Riley uses specific words that make her writing clear and fun to read.

General Words (not clear)
A boy came into the room.
Specific Words (clear)
Marcus tiptoed into the kitchen.

Sentence Fluency

Use different lengths of sentences.

Jackson makes sure to use short and long sentences.

Rex barked. (short) He saw a rabbit and chased it across the yard. (long)

| Conventions | **Follow the rules for writing.** |

Before Mia publishes her writing, she checks for capitalization, punctuation, and spelling. She uses a checklist to help her.

Did you check?

Capitalization

✔ 1. Did you start each sentence with a capital letter?

✔ 2. Did you capitalize the first letter of names?

Punctuation

✔ 3. Did you end each sentence with the correct punctuation mark?

Spelling

✔ 4. Did you spell all your words correctly?

Whenever you write, use the **six traits of good writing.**

Conventions Follow the rules for writing.

Students will use revising and editing checklists throughout the book. They should put a check mark next to a question only when they are sure that the answer is "yes." Consider introducing checklists only after students have made at least one editing (or revising) pass on a piece of writing.

If students wrote a story about an animal (SE page 23), have them exchange stories with a partner and practice using the editing checklist. Provide photocopies of the reproducible Editing Checklist (TE page 516), and have partners answer the checklist questions for each other.

If you would like students to learn to use the different editing marks at this point, distribute photocopies of the Editing Practice activity on TE pages 517–519.

Connecting the Process and the Traits

Before moving on, ask students to name the six traits of good writing and to explain in their own words what they are. If they have trouble recalling the traits, review SE pages 20–25.

First call students' attention to the pencil icons that indicate the steps in the writing process. Then briefly discuss how the writer focuses on particular traits at different steps in the writing process. Explain that all the lessons in this book have guidelines, tips, and examples that will show students how and when to use the traits in their own writing.

26

Connecting the Process and the Traits

The writing process and the six traits of writing work together. The chart shows that some traits are important during certain steps in the process.

Prewrite

Ideas	Choose a topic and details.
Organization	Put your details in order.
Voice	Plan how to show interest in the topic.

Write

Ideas	Put your ideas on paper.
Organization	Make your ideas easy to follow.
Voice	Sound interested in your topic.

Revise

Ideas	Change any ideas that could be clearer.
Organization	Change or move parts that seem out of order.
Voice	Change parts that don't show interest.
Word Choice	Change words to be clear and specific.
Sentence Fluency	Change sentences to short and long.

Edit

Conventions	Check capitalization, punctuation, and spelling.

Writing Traits   **27**

Writing Tips

- **Talk with a Partner**

  Talking with a partner will help you gather great ideas.

- **Use Graphic Organizers**

  Graphic organizers will help you organize your ideas.

- **Think About Your Reader**

  Think of your reader to help you find the right voice.

- **Check Your Sentences**

  Make sure your sentences are clear and easy to follow.

Don't worry about the conventions too early in the process. Leave that until you have revised your writing.

Writer's Craft

Writing communities: Have you ever noticed that actors tend to have children who become actors, and musicians tend to have children who become musicians? That's because acting and performing music are group activities, easy to pass from generation to generation.

Sadly, the same has not been true for writers. Great writers don't tend to have children who become great writers. That is because writing has traditionally been a solitary activity.

All that is changing, now. The tips on this page will help you make writing a collaborative process. Writers aren't all alone. In a community of writers, when one child learns a new technique, two or three others notice and learn it as well. In that way, success builds on success.

Advanced Learners

Challenge students to work together to produce a poster to help everyone remember when and how to use the six traits of writing. Suggest that they include one or more of the following elements:

- a definition of each trait written in their own words
- examples of each trait
- a conventions checklist

Have students present their poster to the class. Display the poster in a learning center or other prominent place in the classroom.

Using a Rubric

Students may associate scoring with grading. Make sure students understand that they shouldn't think of rubric scores as passing or failing marks. Instead, they should use a rubric score as a way to measure how well they are doing and to identify traits in their writing that they can improve.

To illustrate this concept, display a photograph of a car dashboard. (Ads and brochures for new cars often show the car's dashboard.) Ask students to identify the picture. Then ask why it is important for drivers to pay attention to the different gauges featured on the dashboard. (Possible responses: so the driver will know the speed at which the car is traveling, and if the car needs gas or oil) Then point out that a rubric is a little like a car dashboard. It helps writers know how well a piece of writing is working and what they need to do to make the writing work better.

28

Using a Rubric

Hana loves to look at the rabbits at the fair. Judges rate or score the rabbits according to their health and grooming. The very best rabbits get blue ribbons, and others get red or white ribbons.

Your writing can be scored, too, with a chart called a **rubric**. This chapter will show you how to rate your writing.

Materials

Photograph of a car dashboard (TE p. 28)

Rubric **29**

Getting Started

At the beginning of each main unit, you will see a "Goals for Writing" page. It shows you goals for four key traits of writing.

Sample Goals Page

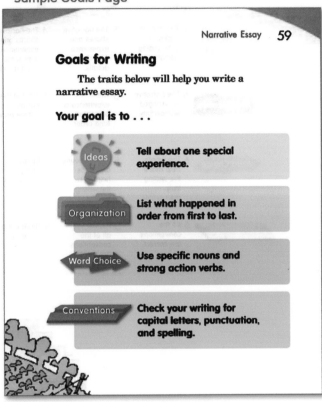

Narrative Essay **59**

Goals for Writing

The traits below will help you write a narrative essay.

Your goal is to . . .

Ideas	Tell about one special experience.
Organization	List what happened in order from first to last.
Word Choice	Use specific nouns and strong action verbs.
Conventions	Check your writing for capital letters, punctuation, and spelling.

Getting Started

Make sure students understand the meaning of *goals* as it is used in the first paragraph. If necessary, provide this definition: A goal is something that you work hard to achieve, reach, or get. Students often set goals for themselves in school, at home, or at play. Share one or two of your personal goals. Then invite students to share a few of their different goals.

After students have a chance to read over the goals for the narrative writing assignment, have them look at the goals for other writing assignments in the book. These include the following:

- Expository essay, SE page 97
- Persuasive letter, SE page 137

Examining these goals will give students a greater understanding of how the traits are applied to different forms of writing. At the same time, it will offer a preview of some of the writing assignments students will encounter in the weeks and months ahead.

Copy Masters

Blank Assessment Sheet (TE p. 31)

Complete Assessment Sheet
(TE p. 31)

Learning About a Rubric

Students need to know how to read a rubric before they can use one effectively. Demonstrate how to read a rubric, having students mimic your actions.

- Point to the number signs across the top and run your finger across. Explain that 6 stands for the highest score they can get in a trait and 1 stands for the lowest score they can get.

- Explain that the traits are listed down the left side of the rubric. To find a particular trait, they read down the left side until they come to that trait. Run your finger down through the traits.

- Next, point to the Ideas trait icon, and ask students to do the same. Explain that for each number sign in the top row there is a description of what a piece of writing has or is missing. Then have students follow along with their finger and their eyes as you read the description for each number score for the Ideas trait.

- Repeat this process for the other three traits shown.

Point out that the rubric provides scores for only four of the six traits of writing. Explain that the rubrics students use this school year will always provide scores for Ideas, Organization, and Conventions. The fourth trait will change, depending on the form of writing.

30

Learning About a Rubric

The information under each number in the rubric below can help you improve your writing. Each trait of writing can be scored.

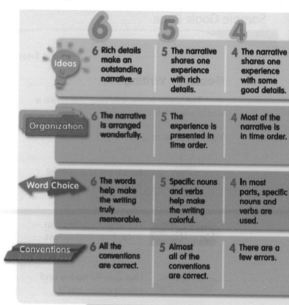

	6	**5**	**4**
Ideas	6 Rich details make an outstanding narrative.	5 The narrative shares one experience with rich details.	4 The narrative shares one experience with some good details.
Organization	6 The narrative is arranged wonderfully.	5 The experience is presented in time order.	4 Most of the narrative is in time order.
Word Choice	6 The words help make the writing truly memorable.	5 Specific nouns and verbs help make the writing colorful.	4 In most parts, specific nouns and verbs are used.
Conventions	6 All the conventions are correct.	5 Almost all of the conventions are correct.	4 There are a few errors.

Rubric **31**

3	2	1
3 More details are needed about the experience.	**2** The experience is unclear.	**1** There is no main experience.
3 Some parts need to be put in order.	**2** The experience is not told in time order.	**1** There is no beginning or ending.
3 Sometimes, specific nouns and verbs are used.	**2** Too many general nouns and verbs are used.	**1** No attention has been given to word choice.
3 Errors may confuse the reader.	**2** Errors make the essay very hard to read.	**1** Help is needed to make corrections.

Talk it over.

1. Which traits are shown on this rubric?
2. Look at the ideas trait. How could you improve the ideas in your writing?

Reinforce the idea that the rubric is a guide to help students improve their writing.

✳ The rubric for narrative writing is found on SE pages 80–81, the rubric for expository writing on SE pages 118–119, and the rubric for persuasive writing on SE pages 156–157.

Talk it over.

Answers

1. ideas, organization, word choice, and conventions
2. Possible responses: You could add more details. You could make sure there are enough details to make the topic clear. You could take out details that do not fit.

Work with students to practice evaluating an expository paragraph. Using the rubric for expository writing (SE pages 118–119) and a blank Assessment Sheet (TE page 499), work with students to score the sample paragraph on SE page 15 (a completed Assessment Sheet is provided on TE page 483 for your benefit).

English Language Learners

Some students may be overwhelmed by the idea of assessing their own writing. Provide time to give each student a personal writing conference, and help them self-assess their writing using the rubric. Model the process using the Think-Aloud approach to help students understand how to use a rubric for their own benefit.

Publishing and Portfolios

Objectives

- recognize the different ways to publish writing
- format writing for publication
- learn about types of portfolios
- learn how to set up a portfolio

Explain that publishing is like getting dressed up for a special event. Just as students want to look their very best at such times, they should want their writing to look its very best for their readers.

Have students say the word *portfolio* after you. Explain that a *portfolio* is a collection of pieces of writing. Tell students that they will learn more about portfolios later in this section.

32

Publishing and Portfolios

Publishing is **sharing** your writing. This chapter tells about ways to publish, including using a portfolio.

Ideas for Publishing

There are many ways to share your writing. Kara reads the story to her class. Denzel puts his writing on the bulletin board.

Materials

Chart paper (TE p. 33)

Magazines that publish children's writing (TE p. 33)

Drawing paper (TE p. 34)

Sheet protectors (TE p. 37)

Markers (TE p. 37)

More Publishing Ideas

Act it out!   Act out your story for your class, your family, or friends.

Bind it!   Make a book. Put your writing and pictures together in a book.

Send it!   Write an e-mail. Send it to a friend, a family member, or a classmate.

Submit it!   Send your story to magazines that publish student writing.

Display it!   With your teacher's permission, display your writing in the classroom.

Read it!   Read your writing to classmates, friends, and family. Sometimes the simplest way to publish can be the best.

Talk it over.

What other ways can you think of to share your writing?

Struggling Learners

As a group, brainstorm a list of publishing ideas and jot them down on chart paper for students. Encourage students to think of other forms for publishing, such as comic strips, mobiles, or posters. Adding pictures to text can help to make publishing less intimidating.

Advanced Learners

Provide students with a list of magazines or online publications that publish student writing. Suggest that students choose two or three magazines and read a few issues to familiarize themselves with the publications and the kinds of writing each generally publishes. As they complete pieces of writing throughout the year, encourage students to submit some of their favorite pieces.

More Publishing Ideas

If students have been working on a piece of writing throughout this unit, help them decide on an idea for publishing it. Have them choose one of the ways described here.

Most students would enjoy posting their finished pieces of writing to a Web site. If your school has an official Web site with links to your class, encourage students to submit their best or favorite piece of writing. If the school does not have a Web site but does have computer capabilities, consider establishing a class Web log, or blog, to which students can regularly post their finished pieces of writing.

Sharing a Handwritten Copy

Students should use lined paper to write their final copy. If the paper does not have printed margins, have students use a pencil and ruler to mark off one-inch margins on all sides of the paper.

Be sure students know how they are supposed to label pieces of writing that have to be handed in. Try to keep this as simple as possible. For example, have students write their name and the date in the top right-hand corner.

Tell students they don't have to add drawings to their writing, but they may do so if they think a drawing will improve their final copy. Explain to students that drawings should always highlight an idea from the story. Ask students which idea the drawing at the bottom of the sample shows. (Some Saturdays we go to the park to kick a ball around.)

Point out to students that they can also add graphs, charts, and diagrams to their final copy to make ideas clearer. For example, if they write about the parts of a flower, they could draw and label a picture that shows the parts of a flower.

✳ For more information about creating graphs, charts, and diagrams, see SE pages 397–399.

34

Sharing a Handwritten Copy

When you write your final copy, remember these things.

- Use your best penmanship.
- Write on one side of your paper.
- Add a picture.

Handwritten Copy

Saturday

Saturday is the best day of the week. My family and I have breakfast together. Sometimes we have pancakes. Other times we have breakfast burritos. Then we might go shopping. Some Saturdays we go to the park to kick a ball around. It doesn't matter where we go. I love Saturdays!

Advanced Learners

Suggest that those students who prefer to write their final copies by hand use a picture book format. Have them determine the best places for page breaks so that they can build the reader's interest. Encourage students to include drawings or illustrations at appropriate places in their story.

Sharing a Computer Copy

> When you use a computer, be sure that your writing looks neat and readable.
>
> - Leave a one-inch margin on all sides.
> - Use a font that is easy to read.
> - Add a photo or a picture.

Computer Copy

↕ 1"

Saturday

Saturday is the best day of the week. My family and I have breakfast together. Sometimes we have pancakes. Other times we have breakfast burritos. Then we might go shopping. Some Saturdays we go to the park to kick a ball around. It doesn't matter where we go. I love Saturdays!

Sharing a Computer Copy

If students will be using a classroom or school computer to prepare final copies, consider creating a template for students to use. This will guarantee that every student's final copy meets your standards and requirements. Be sure to show students how to access the template and how to rename and save the file for their personal use.

Many word-processing programs include clip art with a large variety of pictures in various categories, such as animals, foods, and flowers. Use the classroom computer or a school computer to demonstrate how to insert clip art into a document, or ask a student who knows how to do this to demonstrate the process. Of course, students can also add hand-drawn art to their final computer copy.

Struggling Learners

Encourage students to use a computer to write their final copy. Spelling- and grammar-check features will help students catch many errors that they may have accidentally introduced into their final copy.

Advanced Learners

Challenge students who wish to compose their final copy on a computer to use computer graphics to enhance their final copy.

Understanding Portfolios

Depending on the interest level of your class, decide which kind of portfolio students should keep.

Using a Portfolio

Provide time for students to set up their portfolios. If students will be using a folder for their portfolio, encourage them to create a cover for it with drawings, words, and other designs that help identify the owner of the portfolio.

A folder with a pocket on one or both sides will make it easy for students to store a variety of things.

36

Understanding Portfolios

A **portfolio** is a special place to keep your writing. You can use a special folder for your portfolio, or you can use an electronic file on the computer. Your teacher will check your portfolio from time to time to see how you are doing.

Using a Portfolio

A portfolio can be used in many ways. Here are four important uses.

Collect	You can collect ideas for new stories and poems.
Keep	You can keep pictures and drawings you like.
Store	You can store unfinished writing to work on later.
Save	You can save final copies to read later.

Two Kinds of Portfolios

There are two main kinds of portfolios that you can create.

Showcase Portfolio

> In a *showcase portfolio,* you show your best writing. Your teacher will help you decide which writing to include.

Growth Portfolio

> In a *growth portfolio,* you save writing from different times of the year. You will be surprised how your writing improves.

Talk it over.

> Which kind of portfolio would you like to make? Explain your answer.

Two Kinds of Portfolios

Showcase Portfolio

Establish a regular, rotating schedule to discuss which pieces of writing students should include in their showcase portfolio. If a student wants to include a piece of writing that is not an example of her or his best work, discuss what the student can do to improve the piece.

Growth Portfolio

Make sure students understand that the word *growth* here refers to improving their writing.

Encourage students to save all their work, including prewriting drawings, lists, and graphic organizers, as well as revised and edited drafts. As students review these, they can see or recall what they have learned during the writing process for each writing assignment.

Talk it over.

Students can share their portfolio ideas and plans with each other during the **Talk it over** session.

English Language Learners

Students may be unfamiliar with the word *showcase.* Explain that a showcase is a special box, shelf, or other format used to show off prized possessions. Explain that a trophy case, which students may have seen in school, is a type of showcase. Explain that a showcase portfolio presents their best pieces of writing.

Struggling Learners

Help students see improvement in their writing by having them put together a growth portfolio. After the pieces have been selected, place each one inside a plastic sheet protector.

Then have students use markers to track skills in their writing, such as circling specific details or underlining clear sentences so they can easily see their progress.

Descriptive Writing Overview

Common Core Standards Focus

Writing 5: With guidance and support from adults and peers, focus on a topic and strengthen writing as needed by revising and editing.

Language 2: Demonstrate command of the conventions of standard English capitalization, punctuation, and spelling when writing.

Writing Form

- Descriptive Paragraph
- Across the Curriculum

Focus on the Traits

- **Ideas** Choosing sensory details that make a word picture
- **Organization** Putting details in a logical order
- **Conventions** Checking for errors in capitalization, punctuation, and spelling

 Literature Connections

- **South Korea** by Susan E. Haberle

 Technology Connections

Write Source Online
www.hmheducation.com/writesource

- Net-text
- Bookshelf
- GrammarSnap
- Portfolio
- Writing Network features
- File Cabinet

Interactive Whiteboard Lessons

Suggested Descriptive Writing Unit (Two Weeks)

Day	Writing and Skills Instruction	Student Edition		SkillsBook	Daily Language Workouts	Write Source Online
		Descriptive Writing Unit	Resource Units*			
1–5 WEEK 1	**Descriptive Paragraph: Describe a Person** Literature Connections *South Korea*	40–45			12–13, 83	*Interactive Whiteboard Lessons*
	Skills Activities: • Adjectives		346–347, 470–471	143–144		*GrammarSnap*
	• Common and proper nouns		327–328, 333, 458–459	117–118, 121–122		*GrammarSnap*
6–8 WEEK 2	**Descriptive Writing Across the Curriculum** (Science or Math)	46–47			14–15, 84	
	Skills Activity: • Pronoun (*I, me, we, us*)		336–337, 462 (+)	57–58		*GrammarSnap*
9–10	**Descriptive Practical Writing: E-Mail**	48–49				
	Skills Activity: • Capitalization		418–419	53–54, 55–56		*GrammarSnap*

* These units are also located in the back of the *Teacher's Edition*. Resource Units include "Basic Grammar and Writing," "A Writer's Resource," and "Proofreader's Guide."
(+) This activity is located in a different section of the *Write Source Student Edition*. If students have already completed this activity, you may wish to review it at this time.

Teacher's Notes for Descriptive Writing

This overview for descriptive writing includes some specific teaching suggestions for this unit.

Writing Focus

Descriptive Paragraph (pages 40–45)

In this chapter, the model paragraph describes a person (student's friend). When students write a description, they must rely on their five senses. Before writing a descriptive sentence or paragraph about something, they should write down what they can see, hear, smell, taste, or feel. As they learn to observe carefully, through their senses, students will find the words and phrases they need for their writing.

Across the Curriculum (pages 46–47)

There are many opportunities for students to do descriptive writing in different subject areas. For example, this chapter includes a riddle for an object in math.

Academic Vocabulary

Read aloud the academic terms, as well as the descriptions and questions. Model for students how to read one question and answer it. Have partners monitor their understanding and seek clarification of the terms by working through the meanings and questions together.

Minilessons

Who am I?   Descriptive Paragraph

■ **PLAY** a guessing game. **TELL** children to pick someone in or around the school and, without naming her or him, **DESCRIBE** that person. **WRITE** the following starters to help students use their senses.

She or he looks _____ .
She or he sounds _____ .
She or he likes to _____ .

● **TRY** this game in groups of 6 to 8 children. After a child describes someone, the rest of the group must guess the person being described.

38

Descriptive Writing

Writing Focus
- Descriptive Paragraph
- Across the Curriculum

Academic Vocabulary

Work with a partner. Read the meanings and share your answers.

1. A descriptive sentence describes what something looks like, sounds like, feels like, smells like, or tastes like.
   Tell your partner a descriptive sentence about your favorite animal.

2. A curriculum is a list of the subjects you study in school, such as math and science.
   What are your favorite subjects in your curriculum?

3. If you review something, you study it again carefully to see if changes are needed.
   What do you look for when you review your writing?

The Five Senses   Descriptive Paragraph

■ **HELP** students get a feel for describing by having them **USE** their five senses to talk about the following people. **MAKE** a cluster for each noun on the chalkboard or on chart paper.

mail carrier, doctor, firefighter, noun of choice

● **WRITE** students' descriptive words (adjectives) for each cluster.

What Is It?   Across the Curriculum

■ **LIST** objects from math and science. **HAVE** each student **CHOOSE** an object to describe without naming it.

● **ASK** for a volunteer who would like to have you read his or her paragraph. **HAVE** the class **GUESS** what object is being described. (Objects could be circle, rectangle, snake, ball, tree, thermometer, ruler, bear, and so on.)

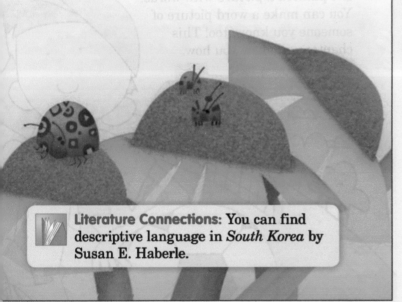

39

In descriptive writing, you use words to create a picture, or image, for a topic. You can tell what your topic looks like, sounds like, feels like, smells like, or tastes like—just by sharing the best words and details.

Literature Connections: You can find descriptive language in *South Korea* by Susan E. Haberle.

Descriptive Writing

Have students play a describing game in which players select an object in plain sight without naming it and then use sensory details to describe the object for other players to guess.

Divide students into pairs and review the game rules.

- Decide who will give clues first.
- Clue giver: Select an object in the classroom that you can both see. Try not to stare at the object.
- Give at least three clues to describe it. For example, "I'm thinking of something that is white and black, round, and has numbers on its face. What is it?" *Answer:* clock
- Add more clues if necessary.
- Switch roles.

This activity prepares students to write the shape riddle on SE page 46.

 Writer's Craft

Description: Here's one way to introduce descriptive writing to students:

"Descriptive writing is like mind reading. I can picture something in my mind and describe it to you, and if I do well enough, the picture pops into your mind, too!"

Then demonstrate this idea using a game. Ask for two student volunteers. Have them sit back to back in front of the class. Give one volunteer a piece of paper and a box of crayons. Give the other volunteer an interesting stuffed animal. Have the volunteer with the stuffed animal describe the animal while the partner draws it. Encourage the describer to talk about sights, sounds, textures, and smells. When both children are done, compare the drawing to the stuffed animal.

Your students will soon see how strong description helps one person read another person's mind.

 Literature Connections

In the nonfiction book *South Korea* by Susan E. Haberle, the author uses questions and answers to describe South Korea for young readers.

Discuss the answer to "Where is South Korea?" Point out a few of the details, and discuss how they help make the paragraph an effective description. For additional descriptive models, see the Reading-Writing Connections beginning on page TE-36.

Family Connection Letters

As you begin this unit, send home the Descriptive Writing Family Connection letter, which describes what students will be learning.

- Letter in English (TE p. 563)
- Letter in Spanish (TE p. 571)

Materials

Poster board (TE p. 39)

Struggling Learners

Throughout the unit, encourage students to share descriptive words they use in their writing. Record their responses on a large sheet of poster board for students to refer to when they get stuck. You may wish to organize the words alphabetically or categorize them by the five senses: sight, sound, smell, taste, and touch.

Writing a
Descriptive Paragraph

Objectives

- demonstrate an understanding of the content and structure of a descriptive paragraph
- choose a topic (a person you know well) to write about
- plan, draft, revise, and edit a descriptive paragraph

Explain to students that a **descriptive paragraph** uses specific details to create a clear picture in the reader's mind of a person, place, or thing. Remind students that a paragraph has a topic sentence, body sentences, and a closing sentence.

✳ For more about writing paragraphs, see SE pages 364–369.

Make sure students understand that a word picture is something that they imagine in their minds as they read. Instead of using a brush and paint to create a picture of a person, place, or thing, it uses words. When people read the words, they see the person, place, or thing in their mind.

Remind students that whenever they write, they are writing for someone (audience)—themselves, teachers, family members, or friends.

✳ For more about the purpose of descriptive writing, see SE page 378.

 Technology Connections

Use this unit's Interactive Whiteboard Lesson to introduce descriptive writing.

🔆 *Interactive Whiteboard Lessons*

40

Writing a
Descriptive
Paragraph

Isabel described her friend Marty in a descriptive paragraph. In a way, she painted a picture with words. You can make a word picture of someone you know, too! This chapter will show you how.

Materials

Audio Recorder (TE p. 42)

Copy Masters

Choose a Topic (TE p. 42)

Revising Checklist (TE p. 44)

Editing Checklist (TE p. 45)

Editing and Proofreading Marks (TE p. 45)

Isabel's Descriptive Paragraph

My Teammate Marty

Topic Sentence

My friend Marty is on my soccer team. He wears a blue baseball hat. His hair is dark brown,

Body Sentences

and his eyes light up when he smiles. He wears a uniform that includes a T-shirt and blue pants. Marty's white shoes wear out quickly because he runs fast and plays hard. Marty loves playing soccer,

Closing Sentence

and he is a great teammate.

- The topic sentence tells who the paragraph is about.
- The body sentences describe what the person looks like and what she or he does.
- The closing sentence tells how the writer feels about the person.

Prewriting Planning Your Writing

To help students choose a topic, distribute photocopies of the reproducible Choose a Topic page (TE page 520). Tell students that good writers usually write about what they know. Suggest that students list names of family members, close friends, and neighbors. These are the people whom they will know best and whom they will be able to describe best.

Tell students that their drawings don't have to be perfect images of the person. Point out, however, that because they will use the drawing to recall details, they should try to show as many things about the person as possible.

To reinforce this idea, have students reread Isabel's paragraph on SE page 41. Ask them to point out details in the paragraph that Isabel may have shown in her drawing of Marty. (Possible responses: blue baseball hat, dark brown hair, smile, T-shirt, blue pants, worn-out white shoes, soccer ball) For more about descriptive voice, see SE page 386.

Technology Connections

Students can use the added features of the Net-text as they explore this stage of the writing process.

✶ **Write Source Online Net-text**

42

Prewriting ▶ Planning Your Writing

To get started you need to select an interesting topic and gather details about it.

First, Isabel listed interesting people she knows. Then she circled the person she wanted to write about.

After Isabel chose Marty as her topic, she created a chart of details about him.

Quick List

Grandma Vi

Anita

Marty

Details Chart

Topic: Marty		
Looks like	Sounds like	Likes to do
big smile red striped shirt blue cap	soft voice giggles	loves soccer runs fast likes popcorn

Prewrite ▶ Choose a topic/Gather details.

1. List three people you know well.
2. Circle one person to write about.
3. Make a details chart like the one above.
4. Draw a picture of your person, if it will help you.

Teaching Tip: Writing Conference

Help students think of details for their details chart in a one-on-one conference in which you ask them to describe orally the person they plan to write about. Point out sensory details they mention, and help them figure out under which heading to list each detail.

Ask questions about the person to generate more details if needed.

English Language Learners

Some students find it easier to express ideas orally than in writing. Have these students use a audio recorder to dictate their sensory details, or pair them with cooperative partners who can jot down their details. Have students play their audio recording or listen to their partners read back the responses so they can write the details on their own.

Struggling Learners

If possible, have students bring in a photograph of the person they want to describe. Have them position the picture in the center of their paper, and list sensory details around the picture. They can use labels for personality traits, such as funny, kind, or smart, as well as other sensory details. Have them use their picture organizer as they write their draft.

Writing ▶ Writing Your First Draft

You can use your details chart and picture to help you write your paragraph. Remember each part of your paragraph has a special job.

Isabel wrote a topic sentence, body sentences, and a closing sentence in her paragraph. She used many ideas from her details chart.

Write ▶ **Write your first draft.**

1. Write your **topic sentence**.

Write your own sentence or use the form that follows.

My friend _____ is _____ .
  (name)   (special detail)

2. Write your **body sentences**. Use words and details from your chart and picture to describe the person.
3. Write your **closing sentence**. Tell how you feel about the person.

Writing Writing Your First Draft

Explain to students that adverbs are words that describe verbs. Point out that many adverbs such as *slowly* and *easily* end in *-ly*, but not all do. Review the sample paragraph on SE page 41. Ask volunteers to find the adverbs that tell how Marty runs and plays (*fast* and *hard*). Encourage students to use adverbs as they write their body sentences.

✱ For more about adverbs, see SE pages 350–351.

Tell students to present details in an order that makes sense. For example, in the sample paragraph on SE page 41, Isabel presents details in order from top (blue baseball hat) to bottom (white shoes). This order is easy to follow.

Technology Connections

Students can use the added features of the Net-text as they explore this stage of the writing process.

Write Source Online **Net-text**

English Language Learners

Some students may become so concerned about using correct wording that it interferes with their ability to write. Remind students to use their drawing and details chart to help them. Point out that they can make changes and corrections during the revising and editing stages.

Struggling Learners

Reinforce the idea that body sentences are made up of sensory details by pointing out that our bodies have ways of telling us what we see, hear, smell, taste, and touch. In a similar way, body sentences let the reader see, hear, smell, taste, and touch what is being described in a paragraph.

Advanced Learners

Challenge students to create attention-grabbing topic sentences so that readers will want to find out more. For example, *My friend Tony is funny* could become *The funniest friend I have is definitely Tony* or *My best friend Tony is hilarious.* Have students share their topic sentences with the class.

Revising Improving Your Writing

Distribute photocopies of the reproducible Revising Checklist (TE page 521) for students to use to make changes and improve their paragraph. Explain that they should put a check mark next to a question only when they can answer "yes."

Have students work in pairs.

- First, have students read their paragraph to a partner. Partners should listen carefully and tell the writer anything that sounds unclear or out of order.
- Have writers make any revisions. Then schedule **writing conferences** *(see below)* before students write their final copy.

Technology Connections

Have students use the Writing Network features of the Net-text to comment on each other's drafts.

✴ *Write Source Online* **Net-text**

Teaching Tip: Writing Conference

Most students will benefit from one-on-one discussions with you about their writing. During these discussions, be sure to praise the student's writing efforts and to convey the message that as a writer, the student always has the final say on what to include and what to leave out of a piece of writing.

44

Revising ▶ Improving Your Writing

Now it is time to review your writing to see if any parts need to be improved. When you revise, check for the traits your teacher feels are really important.

> For her revising, Isabel focused special attention on her word choices and sentence fluency.

> Isabel changed some words and used sentences of different lengths.

Revise ▶ Improve your writing.

1. Change general words to specific words.

> My friend Marty is on my ∧soccer teem.
> Marty wears a ~~hat~~. blue baseball hat

2. Use sentences of different lengths.

> Marty's white shoes wear out quickly.∧because He runs fast and plays hard.

Grammar Connection

Adjectives
- **Proofreader's Guide** pages 470–471
- *Write Source* pages 346–347
- *GrammarSnap* Adjectives
- *SkillsBook* pages 143–144

Common and Proper Nouns
- **Proofreader's Guide** pages 458–459
- *Write Source* pages 327–328, 333
- *GrammarSnap* Common and Proper Nouns
- *SkillsBook* pages 117–118, 121–122

Editing ▶ Checking for Conventions

After you revise your paragraph, check it for capitalization, punctuation, and spelling.

> Isabel and a classmate checked her writing for conventions, using the checklist below as a guide.

Isabel's Editing

My friend Marty is on my soccer ~~teem~~ team.

He wears a blue baseball hat. his hair is dark
                                      H
brown, and his eyes light up when he smiles.

Did you check?

✓ 1. Did you begin each sentence with a capital letter?

✓ 2. Did you end each sentence with correct punctuation?

✓ 3. Did you spell your words correctly?

Edit ▶ Check for errors.

Distribute photocopies of the reproducible Editing Checklist (TE page 522) for students to use to check their conventions. Explain that they should put a check mark next to an answer only when they can answer "yes."

Also, provide photocopies of the reproducible Editing and Proofreading Marks page (TE page 502). Have students exchange papers and mark with a red pencil any problems they see in capitalization, punctuation, and spelling, or focus on only one convention at a time. (See SE pages 401–405.) Then have students return papers and have writers create a clean final copy.

Technology Connections

Students can use the added features of the Net-text as they explore this stage of the writing process.

⭐ *Write Source Online* **Net-text**

Advanced Learners

After students have shared their final copy, they may enjoy collecting the paragraphs in a class album. Invite students to decorate and embellish the album. They may also want to ask their classmates to add photographs or drawings of the people they described.

Writing
Across the Curriculum

Science or Math: A Shape Riddle

Read aloud the sample shape riddle and ask students if they can guess what is being described without looking at the answer (a globe). Have them point out details in the riddle that gave them clues.

Point out the use of the personal pronoun *I* in the riddle. Explain that using the pronoun *I* makes it seem as if the globe is telling the riddle. Tell students to use the pronoun *I* when they write a shape riddle.

Ask students how the riddle is alike and different from the descriptive paragraph they wrote. Possible answers:

- Alike: It has a topic sentence. It has body sentences with sensory details that tell what the topic looks like.
- Different: It describes an object not a person. The closing sentence asks a question instead of telling how the writer feels.

46

Writing
Across the Curriculum
Science or Math: A Shape Riddle

In science or math class, you may be asked to write about subjects you are studying. Ronnie wrote a shape riddle for his science class.

What Am I?

The topic sentence names the helper.

I am a sphere in room 213.

I feel round and smooth like a ball.

The body sentences give clues.

I am bigger than a basketball. Some parts of me are blue. Other parts are brown or green. I have words and lines all over me. I can show you

The closing sentence asks the riddle question.

where anyone on Earth lives. What am I?

Answer: a globe

Grammar Connection

Pronouns
- *Proofreader's Guide* page 462 (+)
- *Write Source* pages 336–337
- *GrammarSnap* Pronouns
- *SkillsBook* pages 57–58

Copy Masters

Sensory Chart (TE p. 47)

Cluster (TE p. 47)

Materials

Chart paper (TE pp. 46, 47)

English Language Learners

Before reading Ronnie's shape riddle, familiarize students with the term *sphere*. Provide examples, such as an orange and a basketball. Have students name other examples of spheres and list them on the board or on chart paper.

Writing Tips

Writing in Science or Math   **47**

Details Chart

Before You Write

Pick an object that has a special shape.

Complete a details chart about the object.

Topic:

Looks like	Sounds like	Know about

During Your Writing

Name your object's shape in the topic sentence.

Give clues from your list in the body sentences.

In the closing, write your riddle question.

After You Have Written

Read your riddle to a partner to see if it makes sense.

Add or change details to make your riddle clear.

Correct mistakes and make a final copy.

Writing Tips

Before You Write

Suggest that students choose one of the objects that they picked for the guessing game (TE page 38) as their riddle topic.

Model creating a sensory chart. Then distribute photocopies of the reproducible Sensory Chart (TE pages 506 or 507) to students, and have them follow along as you read aloud the different headings in the chart.

✱ For another sample sensory chart, see SE page 382.

During Your Writing

To help students get started, provide them with a topic sentence form based on the sample riddle.

I am a (shape) in room (your room number).

After You Have Written

Suggest that students write the answer to their riddle on the back of their paper. Then have volunteers share their riddles.

English Language Learners

On chart paper, draw various shapes (circle, square, triangle, sphere, cube, cylinder, and pyramid) and write the name of each shape next to it. Have students take turns naming objects in the classroom and classifying them by their shape. Then have students choose an object from the chart to describe.

Struggling Learners

Visual learners may benefit from using a cluster to generate details. Distribute photocopies of the reproducible Cluster (TE page 504). Have students write the name of their object in the center of the cluster. Then have them cluster as many descriptive words as possible around their object. Tell students that they can add more circles to the cluster.

Point out that the descriptive words can be checked off as students organize them into a sensory chart.

Practical Writing: An E-Mail Message

Most students are probably familiar with sending and receiving e-mail messages. However, many students will benefit from a quick review of the parts of an e-mail message. Use the sample message as a model as you discuss these parts.

- **To:** tells to whom the message is being sent
- **Subject:** tells the main idea of the message; this can be just two or three words
- **Greeting:** says hello in a polite, friendly way to the person getting the message
- **Body sentences:** the main part of the message
- **Closing:** says goodbye in a friendly way and tells who sent the e-mail

It's a good plan to have students send their e-mail message from the classroom or a school computer.

48

Practical Writing: An E-Mail Message

Paul wrote an e-mail message to his friend Jo. He talked about a park near his home in Florida.

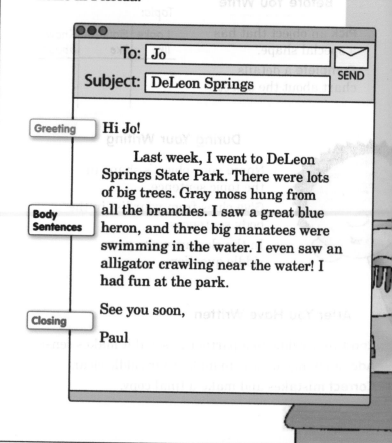

To: Jo

Subject: DeLeon Springs

SEND

Greeting

Hi Jo!

Body Sentences

Last week, I went to DeLeon Springs State Park. There were lots of big trees. Gray moss hung from all the branches. I saw a great blue heron, and three big manatees were swimming in the water. I even saw an alligator crawling near the water! I had fun at the park.

See you soon,

Closing

Paul

Grammar Connection

Capitalization
- **Proofreader's Guide** pages 418–419
- *GrammarSnap* Capitalization of Proper Nouns
- *SkillsBook* pages 53–54, 55–56

Copy Masters

Sensory Chart (TE p. 49)

Advanced Learners

Have pairs rewrite the body of Paul's e-mail message to make DeLeon Springs sound even more exciting. Point out that they can pretend Paul saw other fascinating animals and plants there.

Practical Writing **49**

Writing Tips

Before You Write

Choose a person to receive your e-mail.

Pick a place to describe.

Make a sensory list to gather details.

Sensory List

See	
Hear	
Smell	
Taste	
Feel	

During Your Writing

Begin with a fun greeting.

Share ideas from your list in the body sentences.

Make your closing a friendly good-bye.

After You Have Written

Read over your e-mail. Be sure you have clearly described your place.

Correct mistakes in capitalization, punctuation, and spelling.

Send your e-mail.

Writing Tips

Before You Write

Consider having the whole class describe the same place. For example, choose a place you have visited on a class field trip or a place near the school that is familiar to all students. This will ensure that everyone has a suitable topic. Distribute photocopies of the reproducible Sensory Chart (TE pages 506 or 507). Students can work together to generate details.

During Your Writing

Have students draft their e-mail message on paper. Remind them to list details in the body sentences in an order that makes sense and that will help the reader picture the place.

After You Have Written

Point out that the sample e-mail message does not contain a complete e-mail address for Jo. Explain that most people have an address book on their computer. When they type a name in the "To" box, the e-mail program automatically shows the address for that person. If the person's name is not in the address book, then they have to type in an address. If students plan to send their e-mail messages, they will need to find out ahead of time the person's e-mail address.

English Language Learners

Sometimes students may have an idea about what they want to say but cannot think of the English words they want to use. This can discourage them and prevent them from continuing to write. Encourage students to draw a line to leave room for the unknown word so they will know to come back to it later.

Advanced Learners

Challenge students to brainstorm a list of places they would like to know more about. After choosing a location, have students conduct research, including finding photographs, to gather details for a descriptive e-mail message.

Narrative Writing Overview

Common Core Standards Focus

> **Writing 3:** Write narratives in which they recount a well-elaborated event or short sequence of events, include details to describe actions, thoughts, and feelings, use temporal words to signal event order, and provide a sense of closure.
>
> **Language 2:** Demonstrate command of the conventions of standard English capitalization, punctuation, and spelling when writing.

Writing Forms
- Narrative Paragraph
- Narrative Essay
- Across the Curriculum
- Assessment

Focus on the Traits
- **Ideas** Using details to describe an experience
- **Organization** Putting events in time order
- **Voice** Writing as if talking to a friend
- **Conventions** Checking for errors in capitalization, punctuation, and spelling

Literature Connections
- *My Name Is Gabriela* by Monica Brown
- *Gloria Who Might Be My Best Friend* by Ann Cameron

Technology Connections

Write Source Online
www.hmheducation.com/writesource
- **Net-text**
- **Bookshelf**
- **GrammarSnap**
- **Portfolio**
- **Writing Network features**
- **File Cabinet**

Interactive Whiteboard Lessons

Suggested Narrative Writing Unit (Five Weeks)

Day	Writing and Skills Instruction	Student Edition		SkillsBook	Daily Language Workouts	Write Source Online
		Narrative Writing Unit	Resource Units*			
1–5 (Week 1)	**Narrative Paragraph: A Special Experience** Literature Connections *My Name Is Gabriela*	52–57			16–17, 85	*Interactive Whiteboard Lessons*
	Skills Activities:			145–146, 147–148		
	• Adjectives		348, 470 (+)	147–148		*GrammarSnap*
	• Verbs (action)		340, 464–465	133–134		*GrammarSnap*
	• Prepositions		476 (+)	155–156		*GrammarSnap*
opt.	*Giving Speeches*	300–305				
6–7 (Week 2)	**Narrative Essay—A True Experience** (Model)	58–61			18–19, 86	
8–10	(Prewriting)	62–63				*Net-text*
11–15 (Week 3)	(Writing)	64–69			20–21, 87	*Net-text*
	Skills Activities:					
	• Quotation marks		414–415	39–40		*GrammarSnap*
	• Punctuating dialogue		406 (+)	19–20, 61–62		*GrammarSnap*
	• Complete sentences		353 (+), 354 (+), 355 (+), 449 (+), 450 (+), 452 (+)			*GrammarSnap*
16–20 (Week 4)	(Revising)	70–75			22–23, 88	*Net-text*
	Working with a Partner	16–19				
	Skills Activities:					
	• Verb Tenses		343, 466–467	137–138		*GrammarSnap*
	• Adjectives		348 (+), 470 (+)			*GrammarSnap*
21–23 (Week 5)	(Editing, Publishing, Reflecting) Literature Connections *Gloria Who Might Be My Best Friend*	76–81			24–25, 89	*Portfolio, Net-text*
	Skills Activities:					
	• End punctuation		353–355 (+), 402 (+), 404 (+)	3–4, 11–12		*GrammarSnap*
	• Capitalization		420–421, 449	59–60		*GrammarSnap*
	• Spelling (plurals)		329–331, 422–423	69–70, 73, 74, 77, 78		*GrammarSnap*
	• Contractions		339, 410–411	29–30, 31–32		*GrammarSnap*
opt.	*Giving Speeches*	300–305				
24	**Narrative Writing Across the Curriculum** (Social Studies, Music)	82–85				
25	**Narrative Writing for Assessment**	86–87				

* These units are also located in the back of the *Teacher's Edition*. Resource Units include "Basic Grammar and Writing," "A Writer's Resource," and "Proofreader's Guide."
(+) This activity is located in a different section of the *Write Source Student Edition*. If students have already completed this activity, you may wish to review it at this time.

Teacher's Notes for Narrative Writing

This overview for narrative writing includes some specific teaching suggestions for the unit.

Writing Focus

Narrative Paragraph (pages 52–57)

Everyone has a story to tell! Telling stories about themselves helps young writers see that good stories come from one's own experience. It demonstrates that a writers' most important resource is her or his own life.

Narrative Essay (pages 58–81)

Although students are natural storytellers, they may need help discovering their stories. You could begin by sharing a simple story from your childhood. Let students respond and ask questions about your story. Consider focusing on the importance of a good beginning sentence.

Across the Curriculum (pages 82–85)

Students may use narrative writing in many subject areas. In this chapter, the narrative about a crossing guard and a personal music story offer two examples.

Assessment (pages 86–87)

Tests, especially district or state assessment tests, may include a narrative prompt. This chapter offers guidelines for responding to that kind of prompt.

Academic Vocabulary

Read aloud the academic terms, as well as the descriptions and questions. Model for students how to read one question and answer it. Have partners monitor their understanding and seek clarification of the terms by working through the meanings and questions together.

Minilessons

Author's Stories   Narrative Paragraph

- **READ** autobiographical stories like Patricia Polacco's *Thundercake* or Tomie dePaola's *The Art Lesson* to spark a discussion about ideas to use for writing personal narratives.

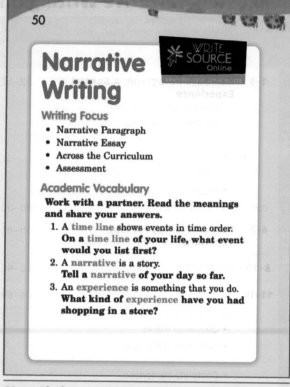

50

Narrative Writing

Writing Focus
- Narrative Paragraph
- Narrative Essay
- Across the Curriculum
- Assessment

Academic Vocabulary

Work with a partner. Read the meanings and share your answers.
1. A time line shows events in time order. On a time line of your life, what event would you list first?
2. A narrative is a story. Tell a narrative of your day so far.
3. An experience is something that you do. What kind of experience have you had shopping in a store?

Story Circle   Narrative Essay

- **PASS** a special object—oversized pencil, ball, and so on—that serves as permission to share a personal experience story.

  - **TELL** students that as they **LISTEN** to each classmate **SHARE** a story, it will trigger story ideas of their own. **ENCOURAGE** students to **JOT DOWN** story ideas as they get them. **CONTINUE** the activity as long as time permits.

Instant Story, Just Add Words   Assessment

- **HELP** students practice topic selection for on-demand writing topic selection.

  - **GIVE** them a very specific writing prompt. For example, **TELL** about your worst cooking (or eating) experience. **HAVE** them **LIST** as many possible topics as they can in 30 to 60 seconds. **TELL** them to **CIRCLE** their best topic idea.

  - **REPEAT** this activity with a variety of specific narrative prompts. **INVITE** students to suggest possible prompts.

51

You like to tell stories about interesting or important things that happen to you, right? When you write those stories down, they're called narratives. In a narrative, you can tell what happened two years ago or what happened just last night. This section will help you write great narratives.

Literature Connections: You can find narrative writing in *My Name is Gabriela* by Monica Brown.

Narrative Writing

Explain that a **narrative** is a story. If the story is about something that actually happened to the writer, it's called a *personal narrative.*

Discuss the term *narrative* to broaden students' vocabularies.

- Ask if students have noticed that sometimes in movies a voice explains what is happening on the screen. This character (who may only show up as the voice) is called a *narrator.*
- Explain that, in books, the *narrator* is the person who tells the story. Sometimes one of the characters in the story describes what happens. Sometimes the author tells the story. That's what students will do as they write for this section. They will be the *narrator* for their *narrative.*

Remind students that the purpose of a narrative is to tell a story. A story can also have a purpose. It may entertain, inspire, or even teach a lesson.

✳ For more about the purpose of narrative writing, see SE page 386.

Literature Connections

Narratives: The personal narrative is one of the easiest types of writing because it focuses on the writer's experiences. Having students write personal narratives is a great way to get them excited about writing and help them develop their own voices.

In the personal narrative *My Name is Gabriela* by Monica Brown, the narrator describes her childhood in Chile, where she developed a love of words and the stories she could create with them. In the end, readers learn that the narrative is about Gabriela Mistral, who won the Nobel Prize for Literature in 1945.

Discuss elements that make the story a good narrative, such as natural voice, interesting details, and personal feelings, and time order. For additional narrative models, see the Reading-Writing Connections beginning on page TE-36.

Family Connection Letters

As you begin this unit, send home the Narrative Writing Family Connection letter, which describes what students will be learning.

- Letter in English (TE page 564)
- Letter in Spanish (TE page 572)

Struggling Learners

Students often have difficulty recalling everyday events. Suggest that students keep a list of things that have happened to them. Have them revisit their lists throughout the year when they need to find a topic to write about for a personal narrative.

Writing a Narrative Paragraph

Objectives

- understand the content and structure of a narrative paragraph
- select a personal experience to write about
- plan, write, revise, and edit a narrative paragraph

Remind students that a paragraph is a group of sentences about a specific topic. A **narrative paragraph** tells a brief story.

❋ For more about writing paragraphs, see SE pages 364–369.

Have students read the model on SE page 53. Ask what made the zoo fun for Colin (seeing the animals, spending time with his brother).

Model the process of choosing a topic by telling students briefly about two or three times when you did something really fun. Describe what you would ask yourself if you had to choose one of those events to write a paragraph about. Possible questions:

- Which event was the most fun to me?
- Which story would be the most fun for others to read?

 Technology Connections

Use this unit's Interactive Whiteboard Lesson to introduce narrative writing.

❋ *Interactive Whiteboard Lessons*

52

Writing a Narrative Paragraph

The students in Colin's class talked about special experiences. They discovered many stories that they could tell about themselves, their families, and their friends. Colin remembered visiting the zoo with his brother and decided to write a narrative paragraph about it.

In this chapter, you will write a paragraph about a special experience you've had.

Materials
Photo of a prairie dog (TE p. 53)
Glue (TE p. 55)
Scissors (TE p. 55)

Copy Masters
Time Line (TE p. 55)
Revising and Editing Checklist (TE p. 57)

Colin's Narrative Paragraph

Narrative Paragraph   53

My Zoo Surprise

Topic Sentence

My big brother and I had fun at the zoo. The peacocks squawked and fanned out their tails. Prairie

Body Sentences

dogs chased each other and dived into their holes. Then we squeezed between people to get to a huge window where we could see underwater. Suddenly a polar bear crashed into the water. It pushed its nose right up to the window. My big

Closing Sentence

brother and I were nose to nose with a polar bear!

- The topic sentence tells the main idea of the paragraph.
- The body sentences tell what happened.
- The closing sentence gives the reader something to think about.

Colin's Narrative Paragraph

After reviewing the three parts of the paragraph (topic sentence, body sentences, closing sentence), help students notice the specific details the writer used in the body sentences. Ask students to point out as many clear words as possible, emphasizing how they show the reader the details. These include the following:

- *big* brother (note that the writer could have used the brother's name)
- peacocks *squawked* and *fanned* their tails
- prairie dogs *chased* each other and *dived* into *their holes*
- they *squeezed* through the crowd
- the *huge* window
- a polar bear *crashed* into the water
- it *pushed* its nose right up to the window

Encourage students to include as many clear, or specific, words as they can whenever they write.

✱ For more about choosing clear words, see SE page 24.

English Language Learners

Students may mistakenly think that a prairie dog is a type of dog. Before reading Colin's paragraph, show students a photo of a prairie dog. Tell them that it is a member of the squirrel family. Explain that a prairie is a huge grassy area in which prairie dogs create underground homes.

Advanced Learners

Challenge partners to write another paragraph as a sequel to "My Zoo Surprise." Have them narrate the story as Colin. Ask students to consider the following:

- What did the polar bear do next?
- How did Colin and his brother feel?
- How did the zoo trip end?

Prewriting Choosing Your Topic

Tell students they're welcome to write about an event that happened somewhere other than the locations listed. Challenge them to think of other fun places. These might include the following:

- their backyard
- a friend's house
- the beach
- summer camp

After students choose an event to write about, help them to recall details by asking the following 5 W questions:

- *Where* were you?
- *When* did you go there?
- *Who* was with you?
- *What* did you do?
- *Why* was it fun?

✳ For more about the 5 W's, see SE page 311.

54

Prewriting ▶ Choosing Your Topic

When planning a paragraph, start by choosing an interesting topic.

Colin's classmates named places that they visited. His teacher listed the places they named. Colin chose to write about his trip to the zoo.

List of Places
museum
pool
park
zoo
farm

Prewrite ▶ **Choose your topic.**

1. List some places you've visited.
2. Choose a place and a time to write about.

Advanced Learners

Review the List of Places with students. Point out that *when* and *where* a story takes place affects the characters and the plot of a story. Challenge students by discussing ways that changes in location would change their stories:

- a park instead of their backyard
- a relative's house (such as a grandparent's) instead of a friend's house
- the mountains instead of the beach
- a theme park instead of summer camp

Gathering Details

The next important step is to select details about your topic.

To gather details, Colin made a time line. He listed events in the order they happened. This is called *time order*.

Time Line

Topic: Visiting the Zoo

— I went to the zoo with my big brother.

— We saw peacocks and prairie dogs.

— A polar bear jumped into the water.

— It pushed its nose up to the window.

Prewrite ▶ **Gather details.**

1. Make a time line like the one above.
2. List the main events of your story in time order.

English Language Learners

Students may become anxious about correctly ordering events on their charts, which inhibits their brainstorming process. Have students generate their ideas and write them down on paper, skipping lines between ideas. Have them cut out their ideas, order them correctly, and glue them onto their copy of the time line.

Prewriting Gathering Details

Explain that narratives usually follow time order. Discuss reasons for this.

- It makes it easy to understand what's going on.
- It makes the story more like real life.
- It keeps you interested in reading, because you are wondering what will happen next.

Tell students to prepare a time line. Model the process using one of the stories you told for TE page 52.

Provide photocopies of the reproducible Time Line (TE page 510) for students to fill out with events.

✳ For information about putting events in order with a time line, see SE page 385.

Writing Writing Your Paragraph

Talk about **prepositions** *(see below)* as one way to add details.

Ask students to look at the model paragraph on SE page 53 and find the prepositions in it *(at, into, between, to, into, up, with)*. Provide help as needed. Point out prepositional phrases and ask what information the phrases add to the paragraph. Encourage students to use prepositions and prepositional phrases to add details to their own first drafts.

✱ For more about prepositions, see SE page 476.

To help students get started writing their paragraph, ask them to

- choose partners and tell each other their stories, making the tale as interesting as possible;
- try to capture that same feeling on paper; and
- remember to concentrate on getting all their ideas down—the sentences don't have to be perfect because they'll go back to revise and edit later.

56

Writing ▶ Writing Your Paragraph

Now you are ready to write your narrative paragraph. Use your time line as a guide.

> To begin, Colin wrote a topic sentence that tells what his paragraph is about. He then added sentences that tells his story. Collin closed with an interesting idea.

Write ▶ **Write your paragraph.**

1. Write the topic sentence to tell what your paragraph is about.

If you get stuck, fill in the sentence below on your paper.

I had fun with _____(person)_____ at the ___(place)___.

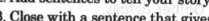

2. Add sentences to tell your story.
3. Close with a sentence that gives a final interesting or fun idea.

Teaching Tip: Prepositions

Explain that prepositions create a relationship between a noun (the object of the preposition) and the rest of the sentence. Among other things, they often tell where or when. To demonstrate, put an object (say, a hat) in various places. Each time, ask *Where is the hat?* Have students respond in full sentences. As they do, write the prepositions on the board. For example:

- The hat is on your head.
- The hat is behind your back.

Then ask students to think of as many answers as they can to a question such as *When do you want to eat lunch?* Have them suggest different prepositions. These might include

- Let's eat at noon.
- Let's eat after our recess.

Revising **and** Editing

Once you finish your first draft, you are ready to revise and edit it. Your goal is to make your paragraph clear and fun to read.

Colin reviewed his ideas to make sure they are in the right order and interesting. Then he checked his paragraph for conventions.

Revise ▶ **Improve your writing.**

1. Be sure the events in your story are in the right order.
2. Also decide if your story sounds interesting.

Edit ▶ **Check for conventions.**

1. Be sure that you use capital letters and punctuation correctly.
2. Also check for spelling errors.

Grammar Connection

Adjectives
- **Proofreader's Guide** page 470 (+)
- *Write Source* page 348
- *GrammarSnap* Adjectives
- *SkillsBook* pages 145–146, 147–148

Verbs (action)
- **Proofreader's Guide** pages 464–465
- *Write Source* page 340
- *GrammarSnap* Verbs
- *SkillsBook* pages 133–134

Prepositions
- **Proofreader's Guide** page 476 (+)
- *GrammarSnap* Prepositions
- *SkillsBook* pages 155–156

Revising **and** Editing

Distribute photocopies of the reproducible Revising and Editing Checklist (TE page 523). Have students work in pairs to check their writing together. Circulate while students are working and check in with each pair to offer help in evaluating their papers.

Writing a Narrative Essay

Objectives
- demonstrate an understanding of the parts of a narrative essay
- choose a special experience to write about
- plan, draft, revise, and edit a narrative essay with a strong beginning, middle, and ending

Explain to students that an essay expresses a writer's own point of view. In a **narrative essay**, the writer tells a story about something that happened to him or her.

Unlike narrative paragraphs that focus on one specific event, a narrative essay will allow students to
- give more details about what happened, and
- tell more of what they felt and thought about the experience.

Assure students who worry about writing a longer piece that as they do the exercises on the following pages, you will guide them step by step through the process.

58

Writing a Narrative Essay

Fred helped his grandpa in a community garden. He wrote about his adventure in a narrative essay. A narrative essay uses more than one paragraph to tell about a true experience.

In this chapter, you will write a narrative essay about an adventure at a special place.

Materials	Copy Masters
Chart paper (TE pp. 59, 64, 79)	Cluster (TE pp. 63, 75)
Drawing supplies (TE pp. 60, 61, 62, 78)	Writing Your Beginning (TE p. 64)
Tape recorder (TE p. 64)	T-Chart (TE p. 67)
Blank transparency (TE p. 70)	Writing Your Ending (TE p. 68)
Sample first draft essay with errors (TE p. 70)	Revising Checklist (TE p. 75)
Dictionaries (TE p. 76)	Editing Checklist (TE p. 76)
	Thinking About Your Writing (TE p. 79)

Goals for Writing

Remind students of the connection between the steps of the writing process and the traits as discussed on SE page 26. Create a T-chart on a piece of chart paper. Write *Writing Process* as the left-hand heading and *Traits* as the right-hand heading. Work with students to discuss and fill in the chart.

Writing Process	Traits
Prewriting	Ideas Organization
Writing	Ideas Organization Word Choice
Revising	Ideas Organization Word Choice
Editing	Conventions

* For more about the traits of good writing, see SE pages 20–25.

Goals for Writing

The traits below will help you write a narrative essay.

Your goal is to . . .

Ideas Tell about one special experience.

Organization List what happened in order from first to last.

Word Choice Use specific nouns and strong action verbs.

Conventions Check your writing for capital letters, punctuation, and spelling.

Fred's Narrative Essay

Invite three volunteers to read Fred's essay aloud, one paragraph apiece. Ask students as they listen to think about what the details in the essay make them imagine. Can they describe the mental pictures that form? Examples include the following:

- a garden with lettuce, peas, and corn in rows
- weeds in the garden
- a boy working in a garden with his grandfather

Distribute drawing supplies and have students draw an imaginary scene from the essay.

Remind students that using lots of interesting details like the ones in the sample will help readers get a picture in their mind of what students describe in their writing.

60

Fred's Narrative Essay

My Day at the Community Garden

Beginning My grandpa took me to the community garden. It contains rows and rows of healthy plants.

Middle Grandpa showed me leaf lettuce, snap peas, and sweet corn. Then he showed me how to pull weeds without pulling the vegetables. It's not easy. He told me that garden work is important. He said, "People who have food need to share it." Finally, we took the food from the garden to a food bank. I felt proud working with Grandpa.

Ending Now I know about growing vegetables and pulling weeds. The best part was spending time with Grandpa. I learned that working together and helping others is fun.

English Language Learners

Students may be unfamiliar with the term *community*. Tell them that a community is where people work, play, and live together. Explain that a community garden is a large garden that people living in the neighborhood can take care of and use.

Parts of an Essay

An essay contains three main parts—the beginning, the middle, and the ending. Look at the three parts of Fred's essay.

Beginning

Middle

Ending

In the beginning paragraph, Fred tells which special experience he will write about.

In the middle paragraph, Fred writes about the experience.

In the ending paragraph, Fred explains what he learned and how he feels.

After You Read

1. **Ideas** What experience did Fred share?
2. **Organization** What order did Fred use to tell about his day with his grandfather?
3. **Word Choice** What sentence contains specific nouns?

English Language Learners

Help students visualize Fred's use of time order by telling small groups to draw a series of pictures that illustrate Fred's middle paragraph in time order. Have students share their pictures. Point out that the pictures tell a story in the order in which the events occurred. Students may use this strategy to organize their events before they write.

Struggling Learners

Point out that the dialogue Fred wrote sounds like something an adult—such as his grandfather—would say. Help students develop an ear for realistic dialogue by having them close their eyes and imagine words that a family member or friend actually said, or would say, to them. Ask volunteers for examples, and write them on the board.

Parts of an Essay

After students answer the **After You Read** questions, talk more about the model essay.

- Point out that this essay's main idea is described in the first paragraph. The middle paragraph focuses on a related idea by giving the details about helping Grandpa in the garden.
- Note that a great way to make a narrative seem real is to use dialogue. Ask students to find the dialogue inside the quotation marks in the model (*"People who . . ."*). Encourage them to use at least one line of dialogue in their essays.
- Challenge students to point out the time-order words used to help clarify the order of events (*Then, Finally, Now*).

After You Read
Answers

Ideas 1. a day at his grandfather's community garden

Organization 2. time order

Word Choice 3. Grandpa showed me leaf lettuce, snap peas, and sweet corn.

Prewriting Choosing a Topic

To get students thinking about their own topics, have them look again at the essay on SE page 60. What was special for the writer about the experience? Possible responses:

- He learned about gardening.
- He helped people by taking food to a shelter.
- He got to spend time with his grandfather.

Explain that it is fine to have only one reason why their experience is special. They might think of others as they write.

Talk students through the process of choosing a topic:

- Write a sentence starter on the board:
  I'll never forget the time I was at _____ because . . .
- Ask students to complete the starter for two or three different places they've visited. Then have them reread the sentences, and ask:
  □ Which experience would be the most fun to write about?
  □ Can I remember enough about what happened to tell the story?

Technology Connections

Students can use the added features of the Net-text as they explore this stage of the writing process.

Write Source Online Net-text

62

Prewriting ▶ Choosing a Topic

Choosing a topic is the important first step when planning a narrative. Always select a writing topic that really interests you.

Here's how Kelsey selected her topic.

List Kelsey listed places she had been.

Circle She then circled the topic she wanted to write about.

List of Places

hospital

Standing Rock

Navy Pier

zoo

Prewrite ▶ **Choose a topic.**

1. List places you have visited.
2. Circle the place you want to write about.

English Language Learners

A limited vocabulary may cause students to be visual learners. You may have students draw a picture of the special place they have chosen to write about. Point out that if they are unable to draw a vivid picture to use as they write, they may want to choose a different topic.

Gathering Details

Before writing, it is important to collect details about your topic.

This is how Kelsey collected her details.

Make Kelsey made a cluster.

Name She named her topic in the middle of her cluster. Then she added details.

Details Cluster

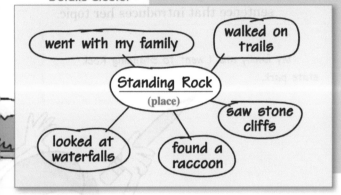

```
went with my family          walked on
                               trails

        Standing Rock
           (place)
                              saw stone
                                cliffs
  looked at        found a
  waterfalls       raccoon
```

Prewrite ▶ Gather details.

1. Make a cluster.
2. Name your topic and add details about it.

Prewriting Gathering Details

Before students make a details cluster, have them close their eyes and think about the story they plan to tell. Help them to imagine the setting as vividly as possible by asking the following:

- What kind of place is it? (A city? A house? The mountains?)
- What is it called?
- What do you see? (What objects? What people?)
- What time is it?
- What day? What season?

Tell students they don't have to use all the details these questions bring to mind, but the imaginative work they've done will give them many good details to choose from.

To demonstrate detail gathering in action, use an idea of your own to create a details cluster on the board. Note that Kelsey phrased her ideas as if they were what she was thinking during the experience. Encourage students to do the same and distribute photocopies of the reproducible Cluster (TE page 504) for their use.

Writing Beginning Your Story

Explain that a good beginning makes readers want to read more. Discuss the samples. Possible responses:

- *We were walking along . . .* : Jumps into the action of the story.
- *Last summer my family and I . . .* : Makes the reader want to know what happened.

Schedule class library time and have partners browse through books to find one with an interesting beginning. Have partners share what they find.

- Why do they like that beginning?
- Do other students like it, too? Why or why not?
- What mental pictures do the opening sentences create?

If students are unsure how to start their essays, you can provide extra support by distributing photocopies of the Writing Your Beginning activity (TE page 524). This activity prompts students to come up with different beginnings.

Technology Connections

Students can use the added features of the Net-text as they explore this stage of the writing process.

✳ *Write Source Online* **Net-text**

64

Writing ▶ Beginning Your Story

The beginning part of a narrative should get the reader's interest and introduce your topic.

This is what Kelsey did to write the beginning of her story.

Beginning
Middle
Ending

Review   Kelsey reviewed the ideas in her cluster.

Write   Then Kelsey wrote a beginning sentence that introduces her topic.

>
> My family and I went to Standing Rock state park.
>
> Standing Rock

Add   Next, Kelsey wrote more sentences to help introduce her topic.

English Language Learners

Students' writing may not sound natural because their writing skills are not as fully developed as their speaking skills. Help students develop their writing voice by having them tell their narrative to a trusted partner or dictate it into a tape recorder. Have them play back their recording, pausing periodically to write down what they hear.

Struggling Learners

Some students may find starting a narrative is difficult. Provide support by offering additional strategies for beginning a narrative, such as

- asking a question
- writing a funny or surprising statement
- using interesting dialogue

On a sheet of chart paper, list each strategy and provide examples. Post the narrative starters on the wall or in a writing center as a reference for students to use whenever they need a strategy to begin a piece of writing.

Kelsey's beginning paragraph introduces her topic and leads up to the main action in her story.

Kelsey's Beginning Paragraph

My family and I went to Standing Rock state park. Waterfalls fell over some of the high rocks. We were walking along the trail through stone clifs. I saw fuzzy green stuff on the edge of the path Then I yelled, "I hear something really strange!"

Write ▶ Begin your story.

1. Write an interesting sentence to introduce your topic.
2. Add more sentences to help introduce the topic.

Kelsey's Beginning Paragraph

After students have read the sample paragraph, draw their attention to the last sentence. Note that in some situations the word *something* would be too general, but here it works well. Why? (The writer creates suspense by keeping what she heard a secret until the second paragraph.)

To help students remember to include all their ideas,

- remind them of the exercise they did for TE page 60, in which they imagined the details of the story's setting;
- have them place their topic list and their cluster list on their desk so they are easy to look at while they write;
- tell them to write the three words *where, when,* and *who* at the top of their paper;
- ask them to cross off each question word as they address it; and
- encourage them to be specific by trying to give names of people and places and tell the day or season when the event happened.

✱ For more about narrative voice, see SE page 386.

Grammar Connection

Quotation Marks
- **Proofreader's Guide** pages 414–415
- *GrammarSnap* Quotation Marks
- *SkillsBook* pages 39–40

Punctuating Dialogue
- **Proofreader's Guide** page 406 (+)
- *GrammarSnap* Quotation Marks
- *SkillsBook* pages 19–20, 61–62

Complete Sentences
- **Proofreader's Guide** pages 449 (+), 450 (+), 452 (+)
- *Write Source* pages 353 (+), 354 (+), 355 (+)
- *GrammarSnap* Complete Sentences

Advanced Learners

Challenge students to reread Kelsey's beginning paragraph and suggest where she could add more vivid details and replace vague words with clearer ones. Have students share their ideas and then turn to SE page 75 to see how Kelsey revised her story. As a group, discuss how students' suggestions are similar to or different from Kelsey's changes.

Writing Continuing Your Story

Share examples of stories with **dialogue** (*see below*), so that students can become more familiar with how it is presented and how it helps make writing lifelike. Suggest that students plan to have only one person speak in this essay because

- they are focusing on including plenty of descriptive details and
- they are working on a short essay.

Have students review the sample essay on SE page 60 and describe how the dialogue is punctuated. Help them as needed.

- The speaker's actual words are placed between quotation marks.
- The dialogue and speaker tag (the words that tell who's speaking) are separated by a comma.
- The first word of the dialogue begins with a capital letter, even if it's not at the start of the sentence.

✱ For information about using quotation marks, see SE page 414.

66

Writing ▶ Continuing Your Story

In the middle part of your narrative, you should tell about the main action. Make this part exciting!

This is what Kelsey did to continue her story.

Beginning
▶ Middle
Ending

Review Kelsey again looked at her cluster for ideas to include in the middle part of her story.

Write Next, she wrote about the main action.

Include Kelsey included details, dialogue (talking), and personal feelings.

I used quotation marks to show that someone is talking.

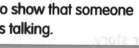

In the middle paragraph, Kelsey included details, dialogue, and her personal feelings.

Kelsey's Middle Paragraph

Inside a garbage can, I found a raccoon. We see wild animals in our backyard. "There's a baby raccoon here!" I shouted. I was mad because no one beleved me. Who cared about seeing another waterfall? I wanted to help the little raccoon. Dad and Mom just wanted to keep walking.

Write ▶ Continue your story.

1. Review your cluster for ideas.
2. Write about the main action of your story.
3. Include details, dialogue, and personal feelings.

English Language Learners

Students have a much larger range of words and phrases to describe their feelings in their first language. Distribute a photocopy of the reproducible T-Chart (TE page 503) and have students list these words and phrases in the left column.

Then ask students to explain when they would feel the way these words describe and help students to translate the words into English. Have them write the English equivalents in the right column to refer to as they write.

Kelsey's Middle Paragraph

Before students start on their own paragraphs, have them look at the sample to see if the writer followed all the instructions. Challenge them to tell how the writer addressed each item.

- Details from the cluster (SE page 63) about waterfalls and the raccoon are included.
- Events are described as they happened (in time order).
- Sentences that describe feelings are
  . . . I shouted.
  I was mad . . . .
  Who cared about . . . ?
  I wanted to help . . . .
- A quotation is, "There's a baby raccoon here!"

Remind students that time-order words can help describe events in a sequence. (They will find a few—*then, finally, then*—in the first and last paragraphs.) Ask students to think of as many time-order words as they can and call them out as you write them on the board.

✱ For a list of time-order words, see SE page 395.

Writing Ending Your Story

Explain that the closing of an essay should say one last interesting thing that ties everything up and makes the reader feel satisfied.

Talk about why telling what they learned from an experience makes a satisfying ending.

- It explains why the experience was special to the writer.
- It can help the reader learn without having to go through the same experience.
- It helps the reader connect with the writer.

To help students understand "the final idea," remind them that after they read stories and books, they are often asked if the writer is sharing a lesson or message about life. Invite students to consider whether their stories have a special lesson or message to share. Challenge them to state it in one sentence.

Distribute photocopies of the reproducible Writing Your Ending page (TE page 525) for students to use to plan their ending.

68

Writing ▶ Ending Your Story

In the ending part, you should finish your story and tell one last important thing.

Beginning
Middle
▶ Ending

This is what Kelsey did to write her ending.

Write   Kelsey finished her story by telling how the main action ended.

Add   Kelsey added her last sentence. She tried three ways to write it.

1. **Say something about yourself.**

   I learned I could be a hero!

2. **Say something about other people.**

   Park workers have an important job.

3. **State the final idea about the topic.**

   Wild animals like to be free.

Narrative Essay   69

Kelsey's ending paragraph completes her story and shares a final idea.

Kelsey's Ending Paragraph

> We finally got back from hiking. Dad looked in the garbage can and saw my raccoon! Then he found a park worker. She tipped the can over and the raccoon hurried into the woods. I learned that I could be a hero!

In my last sentence, I decided to share what I learned about myself.

Write ▶ **End your story.**

1. Write the final part to finish your story.
2. Add one more sentence to complete the narrative.

Kelsey's Ending Paragraph

When approaching the ending paragraph, students may prefer to finish telling their story before deciding on a closing sentence. Others may have an idea for a final sentence already. Encourage students to develop the ideas for the paragraph in any order that feels best.

Students may think the first strategy on SE page 68 is the one they should choose because it is the one Kelsey chose. Read the three endings on SE page 68. After each, ask students if that particular ending shows that Kelsey learned something from her experience. Lead students to conclude that all choices would make acceptable endings.

Literature Connections

Strong endings: Select a favorite narrative book, such as *All the Places to Love* by Patricia MacLachlan or *The Listening Walk* by Paul Showers. Read the ending paragraphs to your class. Then ask, "How does this ending make you feel? What does the writer do that makes you feel that way?" Encourage your students to think about different ways that they could end their narratives and the feeling they would leave with the reader.

English Language Learners

Students may find it difficult to reflect on their experience and sum it up. Lead students to write their "I learned . . ." statement by creating a scenario such as the following:

I wanted to swim, but I was afraid. At first my dad held me up. Soon I could float on my own.

Then ask students what they can say that sums up the experience.

Discuss different ideas, such as the following:

- I learned that I was brave, and I could float.
- I learned that Dad helps me learn new things.

Point out that you can draw different conclusions from the sentences, depending on

- which part you want to highlight, and
- how you feel about it.

Revising Improving Your Ideas

To help students get a sense of **what revising is all about** (*see below*), print a sample narrative (with errors) on an overhead transparency and model the revision process, working with the class.

Another way to help students understand the abstract concept of ideas is to play a game of "20 questions." The types of questions that students ask to discover the object of the game are the same types of questions that they may use to revise for ideas in their writing. As partners listen to the narrative, have them think of questions to ask the writer. Just as the best questions in "20 questions" help the asker picture the object of the game, the best questions during revision will help a writer have the best ideas.

Writing Workshop

Throughout revision, encourage students to share their drafts with other writers and ask for feedback. Help students learn to enjoy the process of discovery.

Technology Connections

Have students use the Writing Network features of the Net-text to comment on each other's drafts.

*Write Source Online **Net-text***

70

Revising ▶ Improving Your Ideas

When you revise, you try to make your story better. First, make sure you have used the best ideas.

These are the things that Kelsey did to improve the ideas in her story.

Read Kelsey read her first draft to herself and to a partner.

> Reading your story out loud helps you find ideas that should be changed.

Listen She listened to what her partner said about her ideas.

Make Then Kelsey made any needed changes.

> In the beginning paragraph, I added two details to make my writing clearer.

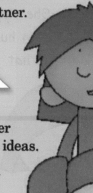

Grammar Connection

Verb Tenses
- **Proofreader's Guide** pages 466–467
- *Write Source* page 343
- *GrammarSnap* Verb Tenses
- *SkillsBook* pages 137–138

Adjectives
- **Proofreader's Guide** page 470 (+)
- *Write Source* page 348 (+)
- *GrammarSnap* Adjectives

Teaching Tip: What Revising Is All About

Many students are reluctant to revisit their drafts, which already seem complete to them. Explain that revising allows writers to fix mistakes, add details, and adjust sentences to sound better. Mention that professional writers revise; every book that students have read has gone through the process of revising. Perhaps the most helpful step you can take to prepare students for the work of revising is to take a break between writing the draft and revising it. Students will be able to look at their writing with fresher eyes. If possible, set the papers aside for a couple of days, perhaps over a weekend.

Narrative Essay 71

Kelsey's Revising

> Last summer,
> ___My family and I went to Standing
>   ^
> Rock state park. Waterfalls fell over
> some of the high rocks. We were
>   narrow
> walking along the ^trail through stone
> clifs. I saw fuzzy green stuff on the
> edge of the path Then I yelled, "I hear
> something really strange!"

Revise ▶ Improve your ideas.

1. Read your first draft to yourself and to a partner.
2. Listen to what your partner says about your ideas.
3. Make any needed changes.

Kelsey's Revising

Ask students to read Kelsey's first paragraph. Have them find examples of good ideas and details.

- She tells who and where in her first sentence.
- "Waterfalls fell over . . . high rocks" paints a clear picture for readers.
- "Stone clifs" is a good detail.
- "Fuzzy green stuff" sounds interesting.
- "Something really strange" makes the reader want to keep reading.

By way of review, challenge students to answer the questions that Kelsey answered as she wrote her first draft.

- When did the experience take place? "Last summer . . ."
- Who was there? "my family"
- Where did it happen? "Standing Rock state park"
- What did the place look like? "Waterfalls fell over some of the high rocks," "trail through stone clifs," and "fuzzy green stuff on the edge of the path."

After students have spent some time revising their narratives,

- invite them to choose a sentence or two they're working on to read aloud;
- ask classmates to suggest a possible revision, perhaps a word substitution or an added detail; and
- let the writer decide whether to make the suggested change.

Revising *Improving Your Organization*

The best order for sharing an experience is to tell about events in the order that they happened.

Also, as students review their narratives for organization, they may discover that an important part of the story is missing. Adding a missing idea may be part of fixing the organization of a narrative.

Another part of organization in sharing a narrative is deciding on the best way to create suspense or excitement. Writers may want to save a special surprise to share at the end of the story. As students revise for organization, have them think about moving some of their ideas to see if the change makes the story better.

After students have spent some time revising their narratives,

- invite them to choose a sentence or two they're working on to read aloud
- ask classmates to suggest a possible revision, perhaps a word substitution or an added detail, and
- let the writer decide whether to make the suggested change.

72

Revising ▶ Improving Your Organization

When you revise for organization, you make sure that your ideas are in the best order.

These are the things that Kelsey did to check her writing for organization.

Organization

Review   Kelsey reviewed her first draft for organization.

1. She made sure she included a beginning, a middle, and an ending.
2. She also made sure that her sentences were in the best order.

Make   Kelsey then made any needed changes.

In the first paragraph, I decided to move one sentence to make my writing clearer.

Kelsey's Revising

> Last summer,
> ∧My family and I went to Standing
> Rock state park. ⟨Waterfalls fell over
> some of the high rocks.⟩ We were
>   narrow
> walking along the∧trail through stone
> clifs.↓ I saw fuzzy green stuff on the
> edge of the path Then I yelled, "I hear
> something really strange!"

Make sure your story is easy to follow from start to finish.

Revise ▶ Improve your organization.

1. Review your first draft for organization.
2. Make any needed changes.

Kelsey's Revising

Discuss why Kelsey moved the sentence in her opening paragraph. Students may observe that it is likely that the family would walk along the trail between the stone cliffs before coming to a waterfall. It also makes more sense in the story to see the family walking along the trail before coming to a waterfall.

You may point out that sometimes changes in organization are a matter of choice. There may not be a right and a wrong way to share the story. The writer is the best judge of whether a change improves the story. Encourage young writers to try reading the story in a different order to see if a change would make the story easier to follow or more interesting.

Revising Improving Your Word Choice

When introducing students to revising for word choice, you may want to play some word games to get them thinking about specific words. A round of "I Spy" could prime their word pumps. Have students take turns in small groups or as a class describing an object in the room until the other students can guess what it is. For example, a student might say, "I spy something that is green." The student continues giving brief clues until the answer is found.

A categories game can be as simple as giving students a general category and asking them to name specific objects in that category for as long as they can: types of fruit, breeds of dogs, toys that don't need batteries or electricity, kinds of birds or trees.

If you wish to focus on specific verbs, invite students to take turns acting out various types of movement. For example, give a student a card with a word to pantomime for the class, such as *march, slink, hike, skip, slide, skate, jump, sneak, hurry, trot, tromp, shuffle, scramble, scamper, hop, stroll, run, dash, plod, bounce, slither, stumble, crawl, leap, gallop, stagger, wobble, weave.* Have the students in the class try to guess the word being acted out.

Revising ▶ Improving Your Word Choice

When you revise for word choice, you make sure that your words are specific and colorful.

These are the things that Kelsey did to revise her writing for word choice.

Word Choice

Review   Kelsey again reviewed her first draft. She paid careful attention to the words.

Mark   She marked the words she wanted to change with the take out (✗) editing symbol.

Decide   Kelsey then decided on better words to use in those places.

In the first paragraph, I changed two nouns and one verb to make them stronger.

Thesaurus

Narrative Essay 75

Kelsey used a thesaurus to find better words.

Kelsey's Revising

> Last summer, parents
> ∧My ~~family~~ and I went to Standing
> Rock state park. ⟨Waterfalls fell over
> some of the high rocks.⟩ We were
>   hiking   narrow
> ~~walking~~ along the∧trail through stone
>   moss
> clifs. I saw fuzzy green ~~stuff~~ on the
> edge of the path Then I yelled, "I hear
> something really strange!"

Revise ▶ Improve your word choice.

1. Review your first draft for word choice.
2. Mark the words you want to change using the take out (⎯⦫) editing symbol.
3. Decide on new words to use in those places.

Kelsey's Revising

Discuss the two word-choice changes that Kelsey made to the opening paragraph of her narrative.

- "Parents" is a more specific word than "family." The word "family" suggests there may have been brothers or sisters or other relatives at the park.
- "Stuff" is a general word that does not create a clear picture. "Moss" is the correct name for the little green plants that grow in moist places in the woods.

Remind students that the best word in their writing is always the word that best describes what really happened. Just because a particular word sounds interesting does not make it the best word for the story. Help students to make good decisions about word choice. They do not need to make changes just to change things. They may only need to change one word, but that change may make a tremendous improvement in their narrative.

Once students are done revising, distribute photocopies of the reproducible Revising Checklist on TE page 526. If you have asked students to revise for only one or two traits, let them know they do not have to check the other trait(s) on the list.

English Language Learners

Suggest that students read their narratives to a cooperative partner or to an aide. Have the listener raise her or his hand if anything is unclear or needs a different word. Offer help as necessary, modeling the process, in order to have the reader and listener both feel comfortable with it.

Struggling Learners

Visual learners may benefit from using a cluster to help them generate vivid words to replace a vague word. Model the process by creating a word cluster. Write *wet* in the center circle and say, "The puppy got wet in the rain." Ask students to suggest specific words that could replace *wet* and write them in the surrounding circles. If students have trouble, suggest words such as *soaked, damp, sopping,* and *drenched.* Then distribute copies of the reproducible Cluster (TE page 504) for students to use to investigate clearer words.

Editing Checking for Conventions

Distribute photocopies of the reproducible Editing Checklist (TE page 527) and have students clip it to their essay. Divide the class into groups of four, and assign each student in a group the responsibility for checking one item on the checklist for every group member's essay. As they pass around their papers, circulate and offer help as needed.

When papers return to the original writers, have them **use a dictionary** *(see below)* to check their spelling.

Technology Connections

Students can use the added features of the Net-text as they explore this stage of the writing process.

✴ **Write Source Online** *Net-text*

76

Editing ▶ Checking for Conventions

After revising your first draft, it's time to check it for capitalization, punctuation, and spelling.

Conventions

These are the things that Kelsey did to edit her writing for conventions.

Check   Kelsey checked her story for conventions. She used the checklist below as a guide.

Ask   She also asked a classmate to check her story for conventions.

Mark   Then Kelsey marked her errors and corrected them.

Did you check?

✔ 1. Did you capitalize names and the first word of each sentence?

✔ 2. Did you use punctuation at the end of each sentence?

✔ 3. Did you add quotation marks around a speaker's words?

✔ 4. Did you spell your words correctly?

Teaching Tip: Using a Dictionary

As often as possible, have students use dictionaries in book (as opposed to electronic) form. This will help them
- practice using alphabetical order,
- become familiar with key words and features, and

- notice synonyms and other interesting words as they browse the pages.

✴ For more about using dictionaries, see SE pages 268–269.

Kelsey's Editing

Last summer, my parents and
I went to Standing Rock state park.
We were hiking along the narrow trail
through stone ~~clifs~~ *cliffs*. Waterfalls fell
over some of the high rocks. I saw
fuzzy green moss on the edge of the
path. Then I yelled, "I hear something
really strange!"

I added capital letters to the name of a place, corrected a spelling error, and added a period.

Edit ▶ **Check for conventions.**

1. Check your story for conventions using the checklist.
2. Ask a partner to check for conventions, too.
3. Mark any errors and correct them.

Grammar Connection

End Punctuation
- **Proofreader's Guide** pages 402 (+), 404 (+)
- **Write Source** pages 353–355 (+)
- **GrammarSnap** End Punctuation
- **SkillsBook** pages 3–4, 11–12

Capitalization
- **Proofreader's Guide** pages 420–421, 449
- **GrammarSnap** Capitalization
- **SkillsBook** pages 59–60

Spelling (plurals)
- **Proofreader's Guide** pages 422–423
- **Write Source** pages 329–331
- **GrammarSnap** Plural Nouns
- **SkillsBook** pages 69–70, 73, 74, 77, 78

Contractions
- **Proofreader's Guide** pages 410–411
- **Write Source** page 339
- **GrammarSnap** Contractions
- **SkillsBook** pages 29–30, 31–32

Kelsey's Editing

After working with students to review the edits made in the sample, draw their attention to the punctuation of the quotation.
- Note that there's a comma between the speaker tag (words that tell who is speaking) and the quotation.
- Point out that using the verb *yelled* instead of *said* is a good choice for the speaker tag. It emphasizes the speaker's excitement, which is already suggested by the exclamation point.

Publishing Sharing Your Essay

Once students have made a clean copy of their essay, distribute drawing supplies and have them illustrate it. Celebrate with a "Special Times" party.

- If possible, share at snack time to create a party atmosphere.
- Have students take turns reading their essays aloud and showing the pictures to classmates.
- After each reading, invite the audience to tell what they liked about the story.
- Finally, award each writer in various categories.
  For example:
  - ☐ funny or unusual experience
  - ☐ easy-to-follow story
  - ☐ natural voice
  - ☐ clean copy
  - ☐ big surprise
  - ☐ interesting title
  - ☐ natural dialogue

Customize the categories to fit your writers. Adapt this practice to many writing assignments. Seek to reward a variety of writing gifts.

Technology Connections

Remind students that they can use the Writing Network features of the Portfolio to share their work with peers.

✴ Write Source Online **Portfolio**

✴ Write Source Online **Net-text**

78

Publishing ▶ Sharing Your Essay

Standing Rock State Park

Last summer, my parents and I went to Standing Rock State Park. We walked on trails through stone cliffs. Waterfalls fell over high rocks. I saw fuzzy green moss on the edge of the path. Then I yelled, "I hear something really strange!"

Inside a garbage can, I found a raccoon. "There's a baby raccoon here!" I yelled. Dad and Mom just wanted to keep walking. I was mad because no one believed me. Who cared about seeing another waterfall? I wanted to help the little raccoon!

We finally got back from hiking. Dad looked in the garbage can and saw my raccoon! Then Dad found a park ranger. She tipped the can over, and the raccoon hurried into the woods. I learned that I could be a hero!

Publish ▶ **Share your essay.**

Struggling Learners

Provide time for students to discuss how a good narrative (story) lets readers know how the author thinks and feels. Read aloud Kelsey's essay, "Standing Rock State Park," pausing at the following places to discuss what the story shows about Kelsey:

- *"There's a baby raccoon here!" I yelled.* (Kelsey is surprised and excited.)
- *Who cared about seeing another waterfall?* (Kelsey thinks that finding the raccoon is more important than pretty scenery.)
- *I wanted to help the little raccoon!* (Kelsey is a kind, helpful person.)

Advanced Learners

With students, brainstorm a list of things that Kelsey and her dad might have done if they had not found a park worker. Ask students each to choose one and use it to rewrite Kelsey's ending paragraph. Have them share their paragraphs with the class.

Reflecting on Your Writing

After you finish your essay, take some time to think about it. Then fill in a sheet like this about your story.

Thinking About Your Writing

Name: <u>Kelsey</u>

Title: <u>Standing Rock State Park</u>

1. The best thing about my essay is

   <u>remembering the baby raccoon in</u>

   <u>the garbage can.</u>

2. The main thing I learned while writing
   my essay is <u>how to use quotation</u>

   <u>marks around dialogue.</u>

Reflecting on Your Writing

Provide photocopies of the reproducible Thinking About Your Writing sheet (TE page 501) for students to fill out.

Have students reflect on what they like about their essay, by recalling comments from both their peers and you.
- They can put the one they most agree with on the sheet.
- Alternatively, are they prouder of something different about the essay?

For the second item on the sheet, ask students to focus on what they learned about the writing process (unlike the essay's closing paragraph about what they learned from their experience).

Have students write the date on their reflection sheet and then clip it to their essay.

Before students place the essay in their writing portfolios, have them take it home to show their families. Encourage them especially to share it with people who are in the story.

* For more about student portfolios, see SE pages 36–37.

English Language Learners

Students with limited English skills may find it hard to say what they learned about narrative writing. They may copy Kelsey's reflection sheet. Discuss their essays with them, focusing on both parts of the sheet. On chart paper, jot down words and phrases students use orally, so they can refer to them when they fill out their sheets.

Advanced Learners

If students feel comfortable with the writing process and using conventions, they may write that they learned "nothing" while writing their essay.

Help them by asking questions such as the following:
- How did prewriting help you write about this experience?
- Why is *voice* a good skill?
- Which revising strategy works best for you?

Using a Rubric

Remind students that a rubric is a chart of the traits of good writing that helps you to

- plan your writing during prewriting,
- make changes to your writing during revising, and
- judge your final copy when you finish writing.

The rubrics in this book are based on a six-point scale, in which a score of 6 indicates an amazing piece of writing and a score of 1 means the writing is incomplete.

Explain to students that they will most likely have different ratings for the traits. For example, they may have a 5 for ideas but a 4 for organization.

80

Using a Rubric

The rubric on these pages can help you rate your writing.

Great!

		6	**5**	**4**
Ideas		**6** Rich details make an outstanding narrative.	**5** The narrative shares one experience with rich details.	**4** The narrative shares one experience with some good details.
Organization		**6** The narrative is arranged wonderfully.	**5** The experience is presented in time order.	**4** Most of the narrative is in time order.
Word Choice		**6** The words help make the writing truly memorable.	**5** Specific nouns and verbs help make the writing colorful.	**4** In most parts, specific nouns and verbs are used.
Conventions		**6** All the conventions are correct.	**5** Almost all of the conventions are correct.	**4** There are a few errors.

Struggling Learners

Focusing on more than one trait may be overwhelming for some students. Hold individual conferences with students in which you discuss one particular trait, such as ideas or organization. Point out ways students can improve their papers and provide benchmark papers as concrete examples of specific ratings (see TE page 86).

Advanced Learners

Lead students in applying the rubric to Kelsey's finished essay on SE page 78. Discuss the categories (ideas, organization, word choice, and conventions) one by one. Read the scoring criteria starting with 6. Pause after each criterion to ask whether students think the essay should receive that rating (6, 5, 4, and so on). Have them explain their reasons by citing evidence in the essay.

Literature Connections: You can find narrative writing in *Gloria Who Might Be My Best Friend* by Ann Cameron.

Keep Trying!

3   **2**   **1**

3 More details are needed about the experience.	2 The experience is unclear.	1 There is no main experience.
3 Some parts need to be put in order.	2 The experience is not told in time order.	1 There is no beginning or ending.
3 Sometimes, specific nouns and verbs are used.	2 Too many general nouns and verbs are used.	1 No attention has been given to word choice.
3 Errors may confuse the reader.	2 Errors make the essay very hard to read.	1 Help is needed to make corrections.

Literature Connections

Gloria Who Might Be My Best Friend by Ann Cameron tells the story of a boy and girl who meet, spend the day together, and become good friends.

Discuss the narrative with students. Does this story remind them of any special days in their own lives? For additional narrative models, see the Reading-Writing Connections beginning on page TE-36.

Writer's Craft

Separate traits: Some rubrics lump all the traits together. These rubrics are helpful for scorers, but they are not as helpful for students. By separating each trait, the student can see which areas she or he does well with—"The narrative shares one experience with rich details"—and which areas need work—"Errors may confuse the reader."

It used to be that students who couldn't spell were told that they couldn't write. By considering each trait individually, however, you can see that someone who struggles with spelling may have incredible ideas.

Writing
Across the Curriculum

Social Studies: A Community Helper

Note that the sample is a narrative paragraph, not an essay, and briefly review SE pages 52–57.

After students have read the paragraph on their own, lead a discussion that covers the following:

- Define the term *community helper* (someone who performs a service for a large group of people or community).
- Tell how a crossing guard helps (the person helps students to cross the street safely).
- Give the story's setting (at a school crossing one day).
- Tell the events in the story in order while you write them on a time line.
- Point out sentences that show how the writer felt (*I felt proud . . .*).
- Find the dialogue in the essay (*"Good job . . ."*).
- Tell why the experience was important (the writer was proud to have helped a puppy).

82

Writing
Across the Curriculum
Social Studies: A Community Helper

For social studies, Josie wrote a story about a community helper. She chose to write about a crossing guard.

Ms. Stein to the Rescue

Topic Sentence

Ms. Stein is our school crossing guard. One day, I was waiting for Ms. Stein to let me cross. Just then, a puppy ran into the street. I yelled to Ms. Stein. Then she saw the puppy, too. She told me to stay where I was. Ms. Stein stepped into the street and held up her stop sign. All the cars stopped, and Ms. Stein picked up the puppy. I felt proud because she said, "Good job, you helped me save the puppy's life."

Body Sentences

Closing Sentence

Copy Masters

Time Line (TE p. 83)

Writing Tips

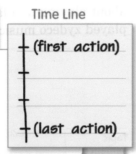

Before You Write

List some community helpers.

Think about an experience you shared with one of them.

Use a time line to gather details about the experience.

Time Line

+ (first action)

+ (last action)

During Your Writing

Name the helper in the topic sentence.

Tell about the experience in the body sentences.

Share how you felt in the closing sentence.

After You Have Written

Review your paragraph.

Add or change any parts to make them clearer.

Check for conventions.

Writing Tips

Before You Write

Have students brainstorm a list of community helpers to refer to as they choose topics. Possible choices:
- police officers and firefighters
- letter carriers
- school secretary or teaching assistant
- doctors and nurses

Provide photocopies of the reproducible Time Line (TE page 510) for students to use.

Ask students to recall words they spoke or thought during the experience they will tell about. Have them write down two or three lines of dialogue, put an asterisk beside their favorite, and plan to use it in their narrative.

During Your Writing

Ask students to refer to their time line and their lines of dialogue as they write. Remind them also to tell *where* and *when* the story happened.

After You Have Written

Take a break from the paragraphs for a day or so. Then have students work with a revising partner and a different editing partner to improve their papers.

Music: A Personal Story

Read the sample paragraph sentence by sentence. Point out that the writer provides information relating to the 5 W's (see TE page 54).

- The topic sentence tells *when* the story happened and *what* the topic is.
- Sentences 3–4 tell *who* was in the band and *what* instruments they played.
- Sentence 5 tells what happened after they began playing (*what*).
- The last sentence tells *why* the experience was important to the writer.

Students may not be familiar with zydeco music. Consider using this as a chance for them to practice doing a little research.

- Have them look up *zydeco* and unfamiliar instruments in dictionaries, in encyclopedias, and online.
- Play some zydeco music. (The NPR profile of Geno Delafose at www.npr.org has audio clips.)

84

Music: A Personal Story

For music class, Richard wrote a story about playing in a family band. The band played zydeco music.

Uncle Bo's Band

Topic Sentence — Last summer I played in my uncle's zydeco band. I played the washboard. My aunts and uncles played **Body Sentences** — guitar, saxophone, and drums. Grandma Kate played the accordion. Everyone got up and danced. It was lots of fun. This **Closing Sentence** — time was special because I played my zydeco music with my relatives.

Copy Masters	Materials
Cluster (TE p. 85)	Zydeco music sample (TE p. 84)

Writing in Music   85

Writing Tips

Before You Write

List experiences you have had with music.

Choose one of the times to write about.

Use a cluster to gather details about the experience.

Cluster

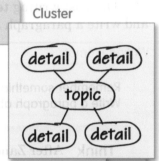

During Your Writing

Name the experience in the topic sentence.

Tell what happened in the body sentences.

Share how you felt in the closing sentence.

After You Have Written

Review your paragraph.

Make sure you wrote about one special time.

Check for conventions.

Writing Tips

Before You Write

Discuss experiences students have shared in music class. Have them choose one of those experiences as a topic or a music-related experience they've had outside school.

Distribute photocopies of the reproducible Cluster (TE page 504) for students to use to gather details.

During Your Writing

Just before students begin writing, have them take a few quiet minutes to imagine and think through their stories. Remind them to

- include all or most of the details on their cluster chart,
- say where and when the story happened, and
- tell what happened in time order.

Encourage students to write the story the way they remember it.

After You Have Written

Have partners work together to improve both of their paragraphs.

Struggling Learners

Many students may not play an instrument yet and may also have difficulty generating ideas about listening to music. Modify the **Before You Write** activity by making a cluster like the one shown on the page. In the center, write "listening to music." Add details by prompting students to offer the following:

- a song that makes them think of a special time
- how a piece of (or certain kind of) music makes them feel
- places they listen to music
- what kind of music they like the most
- songs they like to sing or dance to

Writing for Assessment

If your students must take school, district, or state assessments this year, focus on the writing form on which they will be tested.

In addition to responding to a prompt, this lesson can also be an opportunity for students to practice evaluating a narrative essay. Using the rubric for narrative writing (SE pages 80–81) and the reproducible Assessment Sheet (TE page 499), work with students to score the sample essay on SE page 87. (A completed assessment sheet is provided on TE page 484 for your benefit.) Two additional essays are available in copy master form (see **Benchmark Papers** box below). Again, a completed assessment sheet is provided for each benchmark paper.

86

Writing for Assessment

On most writing tests, you will read a **prompt** and write a paragraph about it.

Writing Prompt

> Remember something you did for the first time. Write a paragraph about the time.

Think   After Zane read the prompt, he thought about things that he'd done for the first time.

List   He listed a few of those experiences.

Choose   Zane chose the experience he wanted to write about and circled it.

List of Experiences

trampoline
high board
soccer goal

Copy Masters

Assessment Sheet (TE p. 86)

Benchmark Papers

The Horrible Day (good)
⬤ TE pp. 485–486

Friday (poor)
⬤ TE pp. 487–488

Writing for Assessment **87**

Zane's Narrative Paragraph

My High Jump

Last summer, Aunt Shandi took me to a pool. Kids in the water were splashing, swimming, and yelling. Then I saw the high diving board. I'd never used it before, but Aunt Shandi said I could jump. I climbed up the big ladder. The water looked a long way down. I took a deep breath and jumped. Down I went. The water made a great big splash around me. My jump was great!

The **topic sentence** names the topic.

The **body sentences** tell what happened.

The **closing sentence** shares a feeling.

practice

1. List first-time experiences.
2. Write a paragraph about one of your first-time experiences.

Zane's Narrative Paragraph

Talk with students about how to approach writing in a timed setting. Tell them they can use everything they've learned about writing narrative paragraphs. Being tested just means they need to consider a few extra things.

- Read the prompt carefully. Read it twice all the way through before starting to write, first to get a sense of the whole question, and again to note exactly what the prompt asks for.
- Follow all the writing steps. Spend a few minutes at the start on prewriting (using an appropriate graphic organizer) and save a few minutes at the end to read the whole paragraph and make revision/editing changes.
- Keep the topic specific, so you can be sure you can cover it in the allotted time.

Have students read the prompt Zane followed. What two things does it ask for? (1) A narrative about a first-time experience, and (2) one paragraph.

English Language Learners

Students with limited vocabulary skills can be so concerned about correct wording that their ability to write their narratives is hampered. Remind them to use an ideas cluster or a sequence chart to help them develop their paragraph. Point out that they can make changes and corrections during the revising and editing stages.

Expository Writing Overview

Common Core Standards Focus

Writing 2: Write informative/explanatory texts in which they introduce a topic, use facts and definitions to develop points, and provide a concluding statement or section.

Language 2: Demonstrate command of the conventions of standard English capitalization, punctuation, and spelling when writing.

Writing Forms

- Expository Paragraph
- Expository Essay
- Across the Curriculum
- Assessments

Focus on the Traits

- **Ideas** Choosing a topic that explains how to do something
- **Organization** Putting steps in the right order
- **Word Choice** Using time-order and place-order words to connect the steps in the explanation
- **Conventions** Checking for errors in capitalization, punctuation, and spelling

 Literature Connections

- *How to Make a Kite* by Joanna Korba
- *Basket Weaving* by Becky Manfredini

 Technology Connections

 Write Source Online
www.hmheducation.com/writesource

- *Net-text*
- *Bookshelf*
- *GrammarSnap*
- *Portfolio*
- *Writing Network features*
- *File Cabinet*

 Interactive Whiteboard Lessons

Suggested Expository Writing Unit (Four Weeks)

Day	Writing and Skills Instruction	Student Edition		SkillsBook	Daily Language Workouts	Write Source Online
		Expository Writing Unit	Resource Units*			
WEEK 1						
1–5	**Expository Paragraph: Directions** (Model, Prewriting, Writing, Revising, Editing, Publishing) 〉 Literature Connections *How to Make a Kite*	90–95			26–27, 90	*Interactive Whiteboard Lessons*
	Skills Activities: • Kinds of sentences		359, 454–455	107–108		*GrammarSnap*
	• End punctuation		402 (+), 404 (+)	7–8, 9–10		*GrammarSnap*
opt.	*Giving Speeches*	304–305				
WEEK 2						
6	**Expository Essay: How to Do Something** (Model)	96–99			28–29, 91	
7–10	(Prewriting, Writing)	100–107				*Net-text*
11–13	(Revising)	108–113			30–31, 92	*Net-text*
	Working with a Partner	16–19				
WEEK 3	Skills Activities: • Kinds of sentences		359 (+), 454 (+)	109–110		*GrammarSnap*
	• Common and proper nouns		328 (+), 418 (+), 458 (+)	119–120		*GrammarSnap*
	• Adverbs		350–351, 474–475	151–152		*GrammarSnap*
	• Verbs (irregular)		468–469	141–142		*GrammarSnap*
14–15	(Editing)	114–115				*Net-text*
	Skills Activities: • Commas in a series		406–407	15–16		*GrammarSnap*
	• Capitalization		420 (+)			*GrammarSnap*
	• Subject-verb agreement		344–345			*GrammarSnap*
	• Spelling		429–431			
16–17	(Publishing, Reflecting) 〉 Literature Connections *Basket Weaving*	116–119			32–33, 93	*Portfolio, Net-text*
opt.	*Giving Speeches*	304–305				
WEEK 4						
18–20	**Expository Writing Across the Curriculum** (Science)	120–121				
	Practical Writing: Invitation	122–123				
	Skills Activity: • Commas		408–409	25–26		*GrammarSnap*
	Expository Writing for Assessment	124–125				

* These units are also located in the back of the *Teacher's Edition*. Resource Units include "Basic Grammar and Writing," "A Writer's Resource," and "Proofreader's Guide."
(+) This activity is located in a different section of the *Write Source Student Edition*. If students have already completed this activity, you may wish to review it at this time.

Teacher's Notes for Expository Writing

This overview for expository writing includes some specific teaching suggestions for this unit.

Writing Focus

Expository Paragraph (pages 90–95)

Today with aerial photos of many neighborhoods on the Internet, a varity of mapping Web sites, and GPS systems in cars complete with calming voices giving specific directions, students may be very well prepared to write directions. Just as a GPS traces one's progress to the desired destination on a simple road map, students will be asked to develop simple overhead maps to demonstrate their directions.

Expository Essay (pages 96–119)

Students enjoy sharing their expertise, showing others what they know how to do well. This form of writing also alerts students to the importance of sequencing when they write or follow directions. Writing is a useful tool for sharing step-by-step information. Learning how to order steps in a process is a valuable skill.

You could begin the unit with an all-class discussion by asking students to share how-to directions for an activity like lining up for a fire drill or feeding a class pet. Number and list the steps as they are given. Then have volunteers try to follow the steps. If they don't work, talk about what's missing. Revise the how-to writing until it works!

Across the Curriculum (pages 120–121)

Another form of expository writing, sharing information about a topic, has application in many subject areas. For example, in this chapter, one student writes a science report about warthogs.

Assessment (pages 124–125)

Expository prompts are a common form of assessment. At this age, students will be writing only a paragraph. Students should learn that the key to writing a good response is understanding the prompt. They must first carefully read the prompt, gather enough information, and then write the response.

Academic Vocabulary

Read aloud the academic terms, as well as the descriptions and questions. Model for students how to read one question and answer it. Have partners monitor their understanding and seek clarification of the terms by working through the meanings and questions together.

88

Expository Writing

Writing Focus
- Expository Paragraph
- Expository Essay
- Across the Curriculum
- Assessment

Academic Vocabulary

Work with a partner. Read the meanings and share your answers.

1. Directions tell how to do something.
   Give directions for making a snack.

2. When you restate something, you say it again, or you say it in a different way.
   Restate the directions you gave for making a snack.

3. If you select something, you choose it from a number of things.
   What food would you select if you went out to eat?

Minilesson

Left at the Chalkboard   Expository Paragraph

- **HAVE** students write directions for how to get from their desks to another place in the classroom (the door, a pet cage, the reading center, and so on).
  - Afterward **ASK** partners to follow each other's directions to see if they find the right place.

First, Next, Finally   Expository Essay

- **TALK** with students about the kinds of things they know how to do. Do they know how to send an e-mail message, draw a picture of a person, plant a tree?
  - **HAVE** each student choose a topic and write step-by-step directions for it.

Prompt Responses   Assessment

- **USE** the reproducible time line (TE page 510) to **HAVE** students **LIST** directions for playing a simple childhood game. (It may be a game students enjoy on the playground or an indoor rainy-day recess game.)

89

Expository writing is writing that explains or gives information. Reports, recipes, and invitations are examples of expository writing. In this section, you will write directions, a how-to essay, a classroom report, and an invitation. To do your best work, be sure to know a lot about each of your topics.

Literature Connections: You can find an example of expository writing in *How to Make a Kite* by Joanna Korba.

Expository Writing

Say the word *expository* and have students repeat it after you. Explain that *expository* is a long, difficult-looking word, but it actually has a simple meaning. *Expository* means "to explain." Expository writing explains ideas so that readers can understand them.

Ask students what makes an explanation—such as directions from one place to another or how to make something—easy to understand. Students may suggest any of the following ideas:
■ giving all the needed information
■ using easy-to-understand words
■ staying on the subject
■ putting ideas in order

These points are the key to good expository writing. Write them on the board or on chart paper and refer to them during the unit.

✴ For more about the purpose of expository writing, see SE page 378.

Literature Connections

In the expository text *How to Make a Kite* by Joanna Korba, readers follow step-by-step directions to build a kite.

Discuss features that are used to put the steps in the correct order, such as time-order words and numbered boxes. For additional expository models, see the Reading-Writing Connections beginning on page TE-36.

Writing an Expository Paragraph

Objectives

- demonstrate an understanding of the content and structure of an expository paragraph
- choose a topic (how to get someplace) to write about
- plan, draft, revise, and edit an expository paragraph

An **expository paragraph** gives information that explains a topic. It may tell how to get someplace or how to do something.

Remind students that a paragraph has three main parts. It has a topic sentence, body sentences, and a closing sentence.

✳ For more about writing paragraphs, see SE pages 364–369.

Sometimes it is easier (and can be more fun) for students to point out the elements of poor writing than of good writing. Read the following directions and ask students to point out why they would be impossible to follow.

Go straight for a while. Then turn at the street. When you come to a store, keep going until you come to our house.

Technology Connections

Use this unit's Interactive Whiteboard Lesson to introduce expository writing.

✳ *Interactive Whiteboard Lessons*

Writing an Expository Paragraph

Directions come in all shapes and sizes. You find directions in cookbooks. You also find them to help you make models or play new games.

To help a new student, Max and his classmates wrote directions to different places in their school. You can write directions, too. This chapter will show you how.

Copy Masters

Revising and Editing Checklist (TE p. 95)

Materials

Chart paper (TE p. 92)

Crayons or colored pencils (TE p. 94)

Max's Expository Paragraph

How to Find the Lunchroom

Topic Sentence

It is easy to get from our classroom to the lunchroom. **First,** you leave our classroom and turn left. Walk past the office. Then

Body Sentences

go to the trophy case, turn right, and stop. Look straight ahead of you to the end of the hall. What

Closing Sentence

do you see? You've found the lunchroom!

- The **topic sentence** introduces the topic.
- The **body sentences** give step-by-step directions.
- The **closing sentence** restates the main idea.

Max's Expository Paragraph

Ask students to identify the following information about Max's paragraph:

- the topic (getting from the classroom to the lunchroom)
- the steps in the directions (leave the classroom, turn left, walk past the office, go to the trophy case, turn right, stop, look straight ahead to the end of the hall)
- the idea that is restated in the closing sentence (finding the lunchroom)

 Writer's Craft

Voice: After reading this paragraph, ask students the following questions:

- "How would you describe the writer's personality?" (smart, cheerful)
- "How do you think the writer feels about the topic?" (confident, hopeful)
- "What do you think is the writer's feeling toward the reader?" (friendly, helpful, encouraging)

Then ask students to find words that help them know all these things. Point out that the words and sentences they refer to help create the writer's voice. Let students know that they should try to sound smart, cheerful, confident, hopeful, friendly, helpful, and encouraging, too, when they write their paragraphs.

Prewriting Choosing a Topic

Have students create a master list of indoor and outdoor places they could go to from their classroom. Write ideas on the board or on chart paper. Besides the ideas shown on the page, students may suggest the following places:

Indoors
- library
- computer room
- nurse's office
- music room
- supply room

Outdoors
- soccer field
- softball diamond
- playground
- parking lot
- basketball court

Students can choose three or four ideas from the master list for their own list of places. Remind students to circle the idea they want to write about.

92

Prewriting ▶ Choosing a Topic

When planning an expository paragraph, begin by selecting a topic that you really want to write about.

Max listed the places that a new student would need to find. He chose to write directions for getting from his classroom to the lunchroom.

What are some important places in your school?

List of Places

gym

office

lunchroom

art room

library

playground

Prewrite ▶ **Choose your topic.**

1. List several places in your school.
2. Choose one place for writing directions.

Expository Paragraph   93

Gathering Details

After you select a topic, gather details about it for your directions.

> Max drew a map to help him remember details for his directions. His map shows how to get from his classroom to the lunchroom. He added labels to make his map clear.

Map

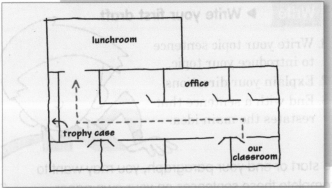

Prewrite ▶ Gather your details.

1. Draw a map that shows the route from your classroom to your topic.
2. Label at least one place you pass on the way.

Prewriting Gathering Details

Explain that a destination is a place where someone is headed. Tell students that if they are going to the lunchroom, the lunchroom is their destination.

It will probably be necessary for students to do a walk-through from the classroom to their destination before they can create their map.

- Group students according to their destination choice.
- If possible, arrange for each group to walk to their destination at least one time.
- Tell them to take notes about which way they go, where they turn, and what special places they pass as they walk. They can use these details to create their map.

Struggling Learners

Explain that just as a street map is drawn from overhead, so is a floor plan. It is drawn as if the roof and ceiling have been removed.

Students may find it easier to follow the path they choose if they turn their map each time the path turns so that they are always facing in the direction of the steps.

Writing Writing the First Draft

Before students begin to write their draft, have them look back at the model paragraph on SE page 91 and help them find examples of the four different kinds of sentences used in Max's paragraph.

- Look for two sentences that make a statement. (first two sentences)
- Look for a sentence that asks a question. (sixth sentence)
- Look for three sentences that give a command. (third, fourth, and fifth sentences)
- Look for a sentence that shows strong feeling. (last sentence)

Encourage students to use two or three kinds of sentences in their paragraph.

❋ For more about kinds of sentences, see SE page 454.

Most students will choose the sentence starters given To Start and To End. When students revise, they may want to add to or change these sentences.

Explain that time-order words help writers show *when* something happens. Have students find time-order words in the model paragraph on SE page 91. (time-order words: *first, then*)

❋ For more about time-order words, see SE page 395.

Writing ▶ Writing the First Draft

Now you are ready to write your expository paragraph. Be sure to use your map as a guide.

First, Max wrote a topic sentence that names the topic. He then explained his directions. He ended with a sentence that finishes the directions.

Write ▶ **Write your first draft.**

1. Write your topic sentence to introduce your topic.
2. Explain your directions.
3. End with a sentence that restates the main idea.

To start or end your paragraph, you may want to complete these sentences on your own paper.

To Start ▶ This is how to get to the _____ (place) from the _____ (place) .

To End ▶ You found the _____ (place) !

Grammar Connection

Kinds of Sentences
- *Proofreader's Guide* pages 454–455
- *Write Source* page 359
- *GrammarSnap* Kinds of Sentences
- *SkillsBook* pages 107–108

End Punctuation
- *Proofreader's Guide* pages 402 (+), 404 (+)
- *GrammarSnap* End Punctuation
- *SkillsBook* pages 7–8, 9–10

English Language Learners

Have students write each of their body sentences on separate strips of paper. Then have them arrange the strips in the correct order and read through the paragraph. If students have made mistakes, they can easily rearrange steps without having to erase their work.

Struggling Learners

Suggest that students search their paragraphs once for time-order words and then a second time for place-order words. Have them circle time-order words in red and place-order words in blue. Explain that a successful paragraph should include words circled in both red and blue.

Revising **and** Editing

Once you finish your first draft, you are ready to revise and edit it. Your goal is to make your directions easy to follow.

> Max first made sure that he included all the directions in the right order. Then Max checked his paragraph for conventions.

Revise ▶ **Improve your writing.**

1. Be sure that you have included all of the directions.
2. Also make sure that your directions are in the right order.

Edit ▶ **Check your conventions.**

1. Be sure that you use capital letters and punctuation correctly.
2. Check for spelling errors.

> Remember to indent the first line in your paragraph.

Publish ▶ **Share your writing.**

Revising **and** Editing

If possible, pair students and have them take turns reading their directions to each other. If the partner can follow the steps to reach the destination, the directions are complete and in order.

If students cannot follow the directions because a step is missing, out of order, or unclear, have writers make revisions before using the checklist. Distribute photocopies of the reproducible Revising and Editing Checklist (TE page 528).

As students edit, remind them to check to be sure that they have used the correct **end punctuation** (*see below*) for each kind of sentence.

Collect the paragraph directions in a class booklet for new students and school visitors to use.

Teaching Tip: Using End Punctuation Correctly

Students may benefit from a review of end punctuation for different kinds of sentences.
- A telling sentence ends with a period.
- A question ends with a question mark.
- A command ends with a period.
- A sentence that shows strong feeling ends with an exclamation point.

Write the following sentences on the board and have students identify the kind of sentence and explain where to add or how to correct the end punctuation.
- This is the quickest way to the office (statement, add a period)
- Make a right turn at the corner (command, add a period)
- Do you know which way to turn next! (question, replace

exclamation point with question mark)
- Hooray, you found it? (exclamatory sentence, replace question mark with exclamation point)

✳ For more about correct end punctuation, see SE pages 402–405.

Writing an Expository Essay

Objectives

- understand the purpose, content, and form of a how-to essay
- choose a topic (a process) to explain
- plan, draft, revise, edit, publish, and assess an expository essay

An **expository essay** is a piece of writing that gives information or explains how to do something.

Assure students that they do not have to be experts at something to be able to explain it. If they know how to do an activity, then they probably can explain it to someone else.

96

Writing an Expository Essay

Emily likes to string beads. Maria knows how to grow flowers, and Ty flies kites. Everyone has a special activity that is enjoyable. What do you enjoy doing?

In this chapter, you will write an expository essay in which you explain how to do something.

Materials	Copy Masters
Index cards (TE pp. 97, 103)	Writing Your Beginning (TE p. 102)
Tape (TE pp. 97, 103)	Cluster (TE p. 102)
Chart paper (TE pp. 99, 112)	Writing Your Ending (TE p. 107)
Markers (TE p. 99)	Revising Checklist (TE p. 113)
Drawing supplies (TE p. 101)	Editing Checklist (TE p. 114)
Sticky flags (TE p. 104)	Editing and Proofreading Marks (TE p. 114)
Student thesaurus (TE p. 108)	
Dictionary (TE p. 115)	Thinking About Your Writing (TE p. 117)
Oak tag (TE p. 116)	

Expository Essay   97

Goals for Writing

The traits below will help you write a expository essay.

Your goal is to . . .

| Ideas | Choose a how-to topic and explain it. |

| Organization | Put the steps in the right order. |

| Voice | Be sure that you sound interested and confident. |

| Conventions | Check your capitalization, punctuation, and spelling. |

Goals for Writing

Writing an essay and working with the traits of writing may seem an overwhelming task to students. Assure them that they will follow easy steps. Remind them that they already used the traits when they wrote their expository paragraph (SE pages 90–95). Discuss the following traits and how they used them in their paragraphs.

- **Ideas:** They chose a topic—a place to get to.
- **Organization:** They used time-order words in order to connect the steps so they could be followed easily.
- **Voice:** They used an encouraging voice to help the reader find the right location.
- **Conventions:** They checked to make sure there were no mistakes in capitalization, punctuation, or spelling.

Explain that now they are going to apply the same traits and follow the same process to explain how to do something.

Struggling Learners

Students may think writing is daunting because they don't connect it with speech. Remind them that telling somebody how to do something and writing about it are similar. Both provide the chance to go back and correct the directions as necessary. Explain that each trait makes the process clearer.

Advanced Learners

Have students set their goal by choosing the trait they most need to work on. Provide each of them with an index card. Have them write the goal, such as *My goal is to put the steps in the right order.* Under the goal, have them list specific ways they can achieve it. For the above goal, they might list:
- time-order words *(first, next, then)*
- step-by-step pattern

Invite students to share their goals and strategies aloud with others. Then have them tape their index cards to the top of their desks or inside their writing folders as a reminder for the revising or editing stage.

Ty's Expository Essay

Read the model essay with the class. Then ask students to read the description of the different parts of the essay on SE page 99. Help students see how each part of Ty's essay matches the description.

Beginning

- It names the topic—flying a kite.
- It lists all the things needed to fly a kite (the kite, a tail, string, a windy day, an open place).

Middle

- Each sentence tells a step.
- The steps are in the right order.
- It explains what can go wrong but tells the reader not to worry.

Ending

- It says flying a kite is fun.
- It gives a reason that it's fun: *You never know how high or how far your kite will go.*

Take time to point out the use of the pronoun *you* in the model essay. Explain that the use of *you* makes readers feel like Ty is talking right to them. It also makes readers want to try the activity.

✳ For more about expository voice see SE page 387.

Ty's Expository Essay

How to Fly a Kite

Beginning   Flying a kite is fun and easy. You will need a kite, a kite tail, string, and a windy day. You should also find a big, open place to fly your kite.

Middle   First, stand with your back to the wind. Next, have a friend hold up the kite. When the wind blows, your friend should let go of the kite. Then run fast and let out some string. If the kites rises, let out even more string. If your kite crashes, just try again.

Ending   Flying a kite is the best! You never know how high or how far your kite will go.

Expository Essay 99

Parts of an Essay

An essay contains three main parts—the beginning, the middle, and the ending. Look at the three parts of Ty's essay.

Beginning

Middle

Ending

The first paragraph names the topic and tells the reader what supplies are needed.

The middle paragraph explains how to do the activity.

The last paragraph tells why the activity is fun.

After You Read

1. **Ideas** What details teach you how to fly a kite? Name two.
2. **Organization** What words did Ty use to put the steps in order?
3. **Voice** Does Ty really like his topic? Name one sentence to show Ty's interest.

Parts of an Essay

Be sure students understand the meaning of *supplies*. Explain that supplies are not always things that you can buy in a store. For example, two of the supplies that Ty lists in the first paragraph of his essay on SE page 98 are a windy day and a big, open place.

After You Read

Answers

Ideas 1. The details are in the middle paragraph. They include the following:
- First, stand with your back to the wind.
- Next, have a friend hold up the kite.
- When the wind blows, your friend should let go of the kite.
- Then run fast and let out some string.

Organization 2. *first, next, when, then*

Voice 3. Possible choices:
- Flying a kite is fun and easy.
- Flying a kite is the best!

Struggling Learners

Help students understand why the paragraph that lists the supplies that are needed comes before the one that explains the steps. Assign students the following scenarios to act out:
- Making a sandwich
- Feeding a dog
- Planting a seed

For students who begin their skits with the first step of the process, ask questions such as *What do you need first? What else are you using?* Help students understand that gathering necessary items in advance makes performing a task easier.

Advanced Learners

Extend the **After You Read** activity by forming three groups (ideas, organization, and voice). Have each group make suggestions for how to improve Ty's essay. Copy Ty's original essay on chart paper and then use a different color marker to incorporate the changes from each group. Post the revised essay in the classroom.

Prewriting Choosing a Topic

Tell students to make sure they choose an activity that they know well. Emphasize that they don't have to be experts at the activity, but they do have to understand it well enough so readers will understand how to do it from their explanation.

Circulate among students as they make their lists and choose their topics. If you think students are choosing topics that are too complicated to explain in a brief essay, provide more guidance on **choosing topics** *(see below)*.

Technology Connections

Students can use the added features of the Net-text as they explore this stage of the writing process.

✴ *Write Source Online* **Net-text**

100

Prewriting ▶ Choosing a Topic

To get started, first choose a topic that you like and can explain.

Here's how Maria selected a topic for her expository essay.

List Maria made a list of activities she likes to do.

Circle She then circled the activity she wanted to write about.

What is your best activity?

List of Activities

wash my dog

grow a flower

play soccer

draw

ride bikes

Prewrite ▶ **Choose your topic.**

1. List activities you like to do.
2. Circle the activity you want to explain in an essay.

Teaching Tip: Choosing Topics

Choosing a topic is the most important part of writing, and sometimes the hardest part. Discuss the following questions and explanations, and suggest that students ask these questions whenever they choose a topic.

Do I understand the assignment?
To understand an assignment, you have to know what kind of

writing you are supposed to do (for example, a how-to essay explaining an activity). You also have to know the length of the assignment (for example, three paragraphs). Finally, you have to know how much time you have to complete the assignment.

Does this topic fit my assignment?
If you pick a topic that is too big, you may find there are too many

ideas you would need to include to cover the topic completely. If you pick a topic that is too simple, you may run out of ideas after one or two sentences.

Will I enjoy writing about the topic? If you don't like your topic, you won't have fun writing about it. Good writers always choose topics that they enjoy.

Gathering Details

To explain your activity, you will need to think of the steps needed to complete it. Be sure that you put the steps in the correct order.

Here's what Maria did to collect details for her expository essay.

Draw Maria drew pictures of the steps and numbered the steps.

Add Finally, Maria added words for each step.

Step-by-Step Pictures

1. pot
2. dirt
3. seeds
4. sun
water
5. sprout
6. flower

Prewrite ▶ **Gather details.**

1. Draw pictures of the steps and number them.
2. Add words for each step.

Prewriting Gathering Details

Have students divide a piece of paper into six blocks, numbering them from 1 to 6, as shown in the sample pictures. Tell them that their task is to show the steps of the activity they've chosen. At the same time, they will be showing the supplies needed to do the activity.

Tell students that their activity does not have to fill up all the boxes. If students discover that they cannot show the steps in six or fewer steps, their topic may be too complex. Encourage them to return to the list of activities they created on SE page 100 to choose another topic.

After students have finished drawing their pictures and adding word details, ask them if there are any supplies that they need that they haven't shown in pictures or words. If anything is missing, they should add it now.

Struggling Learners

Suggest that students look at their series of pictures as though they are editing a video. Have them

- describe each picture aloud and
- visualize what the step would look like in the video.

Point out that picturing the action from drawing to drawing will help them

- put the steps in the correct order,
- uncover missing steps, and
- cut unnecessary details.

Writing Beginning Your Essay

Remind students to think about what would interest their audience (their classmates). Distribute photocopies of the reproducible Writing Your Beginning page (TE page 529). Explain to students that these questions will help them think about other ways to begin their essay. Circulate around the room, providing encouragement to students as they write their topic sentences.

Literature Connections

Strong beginnings: Select some strong expository titles such as *An Island Grows* by Lola M. Schaefer or *What Do You Do With a Tail Like This?* by Steve Jenkins and Robin Page. Then read the opening paragraphs.

Ask students, "How does the writer grab your attention? How does the writer start talking about the topic?" Discuss with your class different strategies for strong beginnings. Encourage students to experiment to come up with their own strong beginnings.

Technology Connections

Students can use the added features of the Net-text as they explore this stage of the writing process.

 Write Source Online **Net-text**

102

Writing ▶ Beginning Your Essay

The beginning paragraph of your essay should introduce your topic in an interesting way. It should also name the supplies needed for the activity.

▸ Beginning
Middle
Ending

This is what Maria did to write the beginning of her essay.

Review Maria reviewed her pictures about the activity.

Introduce For her first sentences, she tried two ways to introduce her topic.

> **1. Ask a question about the activity.**
>
> Would you like to grow a flower?

> **2. Make a statement about the activity.**
>
> I can teach you how to grow a flower.

Add Maria's next sentences named the supplies needed for the activity.

Struggling Learners

For more practice with introducing a topic in a beginning statement, have the group complete an idea cluster. Using the reproducible Cluster (TE page 504), write in the center circle, *Learning something new is _____.* Discuss with students how it feels to learn a new skill, such as growing daisies or flying a kite. Cluster students' responses (exciting, funny, fascinating) around the center circle.

Next, choose a fun skill or activity the class has just learned, such as skip-counting by fives, and repeat the exercise. Record student responses (hard, helpful, a shortcut) on a cluster. Then help them decide which words to include in a topic sentence.

Maria's beginning paragraph introduces her activity and names the supplies she used.

Maria's Beginning Paragraph

I can teach you how to grow a flower. you need a pot, some potting soil, and a flower seed. you also need water and sunlight.

My first sentence makes a statement about my activity.

Write ▶ **Begin your essay.**

1. Review your pictures.
2. Introduce your topic.
3. Add sentences that name the important supplies.

Struggling Learners

Provide practice with using commas in a series. On each of six index cards, write a supply word (*glue, paper, scissors*, and so on). Also make two index cards with large commas and one with the word *and*.

Write the sentence starter "You need _____." on the board.

Have students complete the sentence by taping three supply words, the commas, and the *and* in the correct order to complete the sentence. Repeat the activity several times, using different combinations of the supply words each time.

Maria's Beginning Paragraph

Point out the commas Maria used in the sample to separate the items in the list of supplies (*pot, some potting soil, and a flower seed*). Tell students to be sure to use a comma to separate items in their list, if they list more than two supplies.

✱ For more about using commas in a series, see SE page 406.

Students may recall a supply that they didn't show on their prewriting pictures. Remind them to be sure to add it to their list as they write.

Also remind students to use the personal pronouns *I* and *you* as they write their draft. Using personal pronouns gives writing voice and makes readers feel as if the writer is a friend who wants to share something special.

Writing Developing the Middle Part

Remind students that they can use time-order and place-order words to connect ideas.

- Time-order words will help them show *when* something should be done.

To check that students understand the purpose and use of time-order words, invite volunteers to say sentences, using words from the Time-Order Word Chart on SE page 395. Students can create sentences based on the ideas in their prewriting pictures, which they can then use to write their middle paragraph.

Encourage students to set aside a page of their writer's notebook for time-order words. They can copy the words from the chart on SE page 395 and add more words to each list as they come across them in their reading and writing. Suggest that they use different colors of sticky flags to mark the pages so they can find words easily when they write.

104

Writing ▶ Developing the Middle Part

In the middle part of your essay, you explain the steps to complete your activity. Be sure to use **time-order words** to make the steps easy to follow.

This is what Maria did to write the middle part of her essay.

Beginning
▶ Middle
Ending

Look Maria looked again at her pictures for ideas to include in her writing.

Explain Next, she explained the steps needed to complete the activity.

Include Maria included time-order words like *next, then, now,* and *soon.*

Use your pictures as a guide as you write.

English Language Learners

To be sure students understand the meaning of time-order words, sketch pictures and label them with time-order words. For example,

- make a quick sketch of Ty flying a kite, and write *first* next to the kite; and

- then ask "What is the first step in flying a kite?" (Stand with your back to the wind.)

Continue the process using other time-order words. Help students check for time-order words in their essays.

In the middle paragraph, Maria explained how to do her activity. She used the time-order words.

Maria's Middle Paragraph

Put some potting soil in a clay
pot. Next, make a little hole in the
dirt. Plant a seed. Cover it up with
dirt. Now put the pot near a sunny
window. Then give the seed a little
water every day. Soon, a tiny, green
plant will grow. Be sure it gets
sunlight and water. A flower will bloum.

Write ▶ **Develop the middle part.**

1. Look at your pictures.
2. Explain the steps to complete the activity.
3. Include time-order words to connect the steps.

Maria's Middle Paragraph

Remind students that they are writing a first draft. At this point, their writing doesn't have to be perfect. They can revise and edit their draft later.

- They should use their prewriting pictures to make sure that they write their steps in order.
- They may realize that their prewriting pictures show a step out of order. Then they should renumber the pictures in the correct order.
- They may realize that they are missing a step in their pictures. They can add a picture or a word detail to their prewriting pictures if they wish, but they must write the step in their middle paragraph.

Writing Ending Your Essay

Students will be asked on SE page 107 to give two or three good reasons in their ending paragraph. Help students make the connection between the ways of *telling why* on this page and including *reasons* on the next page. To make this clear, explain that the sample endings on this page are interesting because they give *reasons* that *tell why* the activity is fun.

The first example gives a reason that tells why the writer enjoys the activity. (The reason that the writer likes to grow flowers is because they are pretty.)

The second example gives a reason that tells why readers will enjoy the activity. (The reason that readers might like to grow flowers is because growing flowers is a colorful hobby.)

106

Writing ▶ Ending Your Essay

In the ending paragraph, you should state why you like the activity. Then you should give reasons to explain the statement.

This is what Maria did to write her ending paragraph.

Beginning
Middle
▶ Ending

Write Maria tried two ways to start this paragraph.

1. **Tell why you like the activity.**

   I like growing flowers because they are pretty.

2. **Tell why others might like this activity.**

   Growing flowers is a colorful hobby.

Choose Maria chose the best way.

Add Maria added two reasons that explain her choice.

Expository Essay **107**

Maria stated why she enjoys the activity. Then she included reasons to explain the statement.

Maria's Ending Paragraph

> I like growing flowers because they are pretty. It is fun to watch them grow. When they bloum, I pick them for my mom.

Try to give two strong reasons in this paragraph.

Write ▶ **End your essay.**

1. Write a sentence that tells why you like the activity or why the reader might like it.
2. Add two or three good reasons to explain the first sentence.

Struggling Learners

Before writing their ending paragraphs, have each writer tell their reasons from SE page 107 to a partner and ask the partner to say which reasons they think are strongest. If students come up with more than three reasons, help them to narrow their choices by having them think about those that would probably persuade a friend to try the activity.

Maria's Ending Paragraph

Help students identify the three reasons in the sample ending that Maria gives for growing flowers:

- Flowers are pretty.
- She likes to watch them grow.
- She likes to pick them for her mom.

Distribute photocopies of the reproducible Writing Your Ending page (TE page 530), and have students write as many responses as they can. To help them generate reasons, have them ask themselves these questions:

- What is the main reason I like this activity?
- How do I feel after I have followed the steps to do this activity?
- What is something I've learned because I do this activity?

Revising **Improving Your Ideas**

To revise for ideas, students need to thoughtfully read their rough drafts. However, it is often difficult for writers to be objective while reading something that they have written because their brains supply the ideas that are missing. That is why the role of a partner is so important.

Tell students that a good how-to essay should never leave readers feeling like they have just read a mystery. Have students read their rough drafts out loud for a partner. Encourage partners to think like detectives. When checking for ideas, partners listen for missing information. Ask them to consider what additional clues would help them figure out how to complete the activity. Partners should ask questions beginning with words such as *what, when, where, why,* and *how.*

Technology Connections

Have students use the Writing Network features of the Net-text to comment on each other's drafts.

Write Source Online **Net-text**

108

Revising ▶ Improving Your Ideas

When you revise, you try to make your essay better. First, be sure that you have used the best ideas.

Ideas

These are the things that Maria did to improve the ideas in her essay.

Read   Maria read her first draft to herself and to a partner.

Listen   She listened to what her partner said about her ideas.

Make   Then Maria made the needed changes.

In the beginning paragraph, I added a detail. In the middle paragraph, I made an idea clearer.

Struggling Learners

If reading an essay proves too challenging for a writer, have her or him describe the activity for a partner by using the prewriting drawings.

For a partner whose learning style may be more visual than auditory, suggest that he or she look at the drawings of the activity while listening to the writer reading the essay.

English Language Learners

Help students use clearer, more specific nouns. Have each student choose a noun from his or her essay. Use a student thesaurus to look up each word (see SE page 389). Write each word and its thesaurus synonyms on the board. Help students decide if they should replace their word with one from the thesaurus.

Maria's Revising

I can teach you how to grow a

flower. you need a ‸clay pot, some potting soil,

and a flower seed. you also need water

and sunlight.

     Put some potting soil in the clay

pot. Next, make a little hole in the dirt.

‸Drop a flower seed into the hole

Plant a seed. Cover it up with dirt. Now

put the pot near a sunny window. Then

give the seed a little water every day.

Soon, a tiny, green plant will grow. Be

sure it gets sunlight and water. A pretty

flower will bloum.

Revise ▶ **Improve your ideas.**

1. Read your first draft to yourself and a partner.
2. Listen to what your partner says about your ideas.
3. Make any needed changes.

Maria's Revising

Have students look at the changes that Maria made to her essay. Then ask them what question a partner may have asked to make her ideas clearer.

- What kind of pot should I use?
- How do I plant a seed?

Remind students that they will need to decide which ideas they will use. Not every idea that a partner shares will make an essay better. Usually the student writer will know when an idea improves the essay.

Grammar Connection

Kinds of Sentences
- **Proofreader's Guide** page 454 (+)
- **Write Source** page 359 (+)
- **GrammarSnap** Kinds of Sentences
- **SkillsBook** pages 109–110

Common and Proper Nouns
- **Proofreader's Guide** pages 418 (+), 458 (+)
- **Write Source** page 328 (+)

- **GrammarSnap** Common and Proper Nouns
- **SkillsBook** pages 119–120

Adverbs
- **Proofreader's Guide** pages 474–475
- **Write Source** pages 350–351
- **GrammarSnap** Adverbs
- **SkillsBook** pages 151–152

Verbs (irregular)
- **Proofreader's Guide** pages 468–469
- **GrammarSnap** Irregular Verbs
- **SkillsBook** pages 141–142

Revising Improving Your Organization

To remind students of the importance of organization and time-order words, ask them to complete a simple task, but give them the directions in the wrong order. Hand out blank pieces of paper and ask students to make a special "Happy" note to give to a friend.

1. Tell them to write their note on one side of the paper.
2. Tell them to fold the paper in half from top to bottom.
3. Have them fold the paper in half again from side to side.
4. Tell them to write a greeting on the front of the folded note and share it with a friend.

Then discuss the problems with the organization of the directions. Have them supply time-order words to create the intended note.

- First, fold a sheet of blank paper in half from top to bottom.
- Next, fold the paper in half again from side to side.
- Then write a note inside for a friend.
- Finally, write a greeting on the front of the card and share it with a friend.

110

Revising ▶ Improving Your Organization

When you revise for organization, you make sure your ideas are in the correct order and easy to follow.

Organization

Here's what Maria did to put her writing in the best order for improved organization.

Review Maria reviewed her first draft for organization. She asked herself two questions:

1. Did I put the steps in the right order?
2. Did I use time-order words to connect the steps?

Ask Maria also asked a classmate to check her essay for organization.

Make Then she made the needed changes.

I added two time-order words to make the steps easier to follow.

Expository Essay **111**

Maria's Revising

> I can teach you how to grow a
>   clay
> flower. you need a ∧pot, some potting soil,
>
> and a flower seed. you also need water
>
> and sunlight.
>   First,
>   ∧Put some potting soil in the clay
>
> pot. Next, make a little hole in the dirt.
>   Drop a flower seed into the hole
> ~~Plant a seed.~~ Cover it up with dirt. Now
> ∧
> put the pot near a sunny window. Then
>
> give the seed a little water every day.
>
> Soon, a tiny, green plant will grow. Be
>   Finally,
> sure it gets sunlight and water. ∧A pretty
>
> flower will bloum.

Revise ▶ Improve your organization.

1. Review your first draft for organization.
2. Ask a classmate to check your writing
   for organization.
3. Make any needed changes.

Maria's Revising

Review the revising changes that Maria made
to the sample draft. Ask students to explain
how the changes improve the essay.

- "First" clearly marks the first step in the
  activity—putting the soil in the pot.
- "Finally" signals the last step in the
  activity—when the flower blooms.

Point out that Maria does not use a time-order
word for each sentence that describes a step in
the activity. Students need to make decisions
about the best places to use time-order words.
You might suggest that they try a variety of
possible words to discover which one best fits
a particular sentence. For example, you could
point out that "Now" and "Then" could be
switched in Maria's two sentences. However,
"Then" works better where it is because it tells
about doing something every day.

Once again, you can suggest that students work
with "detective" partners. The student who is
listening to the essay is the detective. This
time, he or she is listening for missing steps in
the activity or steps that might be out of order.

Revising Improving Your Voice

At this age, students often write the way that they talk. This gives their writing a natural voice. When students write about how to do something, they should sound excited and confident.

Invite students to suggest words and sentences that show excitement. List their ideas on the board or chart paper.

- I love . . .
- . . . makes me happy.
- My favorite . . .
- It's wonderful to . . .
- I look forward to . . .
- It's amazing . . .
- I can't wait . . .
- It's incredible.
- Fantastic . . .
- Marvelous . . .
- Excellent . . .
- An adventure . . .

Talk about words or expressions that people use to show confidence. Students may be able to generate some of these expressions, or you may list some on the board.

- I can do that.
- Just do what I say.
- I know how to . . .
- Follow me . . .
- All you need to do . . .
- It's easy.
- I do this all the time.
- I enjoy doing this.

112

Revising ▶ Improving Your Voice

When you revise for voice, you make sure that you sound confident and excited about your topic. If you know a lot about your topic, your writing should have voice.

Here's what Maria did to check her writing for voice.

Read Maria reread her first draft. She asked herself two questions:

1. Do I sound confident in every part?
2. Do I sound excited about the activity?

Ask Maria also asked her teacher to check her essay for voice.

Make Then she made any needed changes.

I added a sentence that helps me sound more confident.

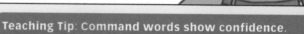

Teaching Tip: Command words show confidence.

Point out that commands suggest confidence. Have students find the commands in Maria's paragraphs.
- revision "*follow* these steps"
- "*put* some potting soil"
- "*make* a little hole"
- revision "*Drop* a flower seed"
- "*Cover* it up"
- "*put* the pot"
- "*give* the seed"
- "*Be* sure it gets"

The most confident commands are the ones that best fit the actions they describe. Discuss the difference between saying "plant" a seed and "drop" a seed into a hole. *Drop* is more specific. It gives clearer information and makes a stronger picture for the reader. Have students check their commands to be sure they are clear and confident.

Expository Essay **113**

Maria's Revising

> I can teach you how to grow a
>   *clay*
> flower. you need a ∧pot, some potting soil,
>
> and a flower seed. you also need water
>   *Then just follow these steps.*
> and sunlight.∧
> *First,*
>   ∧Put some potting soil in the clay
>
> pot. Next, make a little hole in the dirt.
> *Drop a flower seed into the hole*
> ∧~~Plant a seed.~~ Cover it up with dirt. Now
>
> put the pot near a sunny window. Then
>
> give the seed a little water every day.
>
> Soon, a tiny, green plant will grow. Be
>   *Finally,*
> sure it gets sunlight and water.∧A pretty
>
> flower will bloum.

Revise ▶ Improve your voice.

1. Reread your first draft to be sure that you sound confident and excited about your topic.
2. Ask your teacher to check your writing for voice.
3. Make any needed changes.

Maria's Revising

Tell students to look at their papers. They have already revised for ideas and organization, so they probably have some planned changes marked on their essays. Now, they are going to read their essays one more time to see where they could add some words that would show excitement or make them sound confident about their activity.

How does the sentence that Maria added show her confidence about growing flowers?
- The sentence uses the word *follow* as a command.
- She is saying that she knows the steps to follow.
- She has already told about all the supplies. When she says, "*just* follow these steps," she makes the process sound simple.
- When she says, "just *follow these steps*," she sounds like she has grown flowers before.

Once students are done revising, distribute photocopies of the reproducible Revising Checklist on TE page 531. If you have asked students to revise for only one or two traits, let them know they do not have to check the other trait(s) on the list.

Advanced Learners

Invite students to tackle more complex topics that interest them. They may write more than three paragraphs. If particular topics would make good demonstration speeches, invite volunteers to prepare presentations for the class.

Struggling Learners

To help students make their commands more confident, give them the following general instructions. Have them act out each action and ask them for a stronger verb to describe it. Possible verbs are given in parentheses after each sentence.

- *Get* a jar of mayonnaise. *(Open)*
- *Put* some mayonnaise on the bread. *(Spread)*
- *Put* the bacon on next. *(Lay, Place)*
- Then *put* lettuce on top of the bacon. *(add)*
- Next, *put* slices of tomato on the lettuce. *(pile)*

Editing Checking Your Conventions

Distribute photocopies of the reproducible Editing Checklist (TE page 532) for students to use.

Ask students what it means *to indent* (to begin a line of writing farther in from the margin). Tell students that if there's room on their papers, they should indent an inch if they are handwriting their essay and five spaces if they are using a computer.

Also remind students to make sure that they have spelled the names of special people, places, and things correctly. Tell them to make sure that they have used a capital letter at the beginning of all proper nouns.

✳ For information about capitalizing proper nouns, see SE pages 328 and 418.

Distribute photocopies of the reproducible Editing and Proofreading Marks (TE page 502) and encourage students to use them as they edit. Remind students that they can also find these marks on the inside back cover of their textbook.

Technology Connections

Students can use the added features of the Net-text as they explore this stage of the writing process.

✳ *Write Source Online* **Net-text**

English Language Learners

Many languages have sentence structures that differ from those in English. For example, the literal translation of *agua fría* from Spanish to English is *water cold*. However, in English we would write *cold water*. Pair students with cooperative, language-proficient partners who can help them find and correct grammatical constructions, such as these, in their writing.

114

Editing ▶ Checking Your Conventions

After revising your first draft, it's time to check it for capitalization, punctuation, and spelling.

Conventions

These are the things that Maria did to edit her writing for conventions.

Check Maria checked for conventions using the checklist below as a guide.

Ask She also asked a classmate to check her essay for conventions.

Mark Then Maria marked her errors and corrected them. You can see her changes on the next page.

Did you check?

✓ 1. Did you capitalize names and the first word of each sentence?

✓ 2. Did you use punctuation at the end of each sentence?

✓ 3. Did you spell your words correctly?

Grammar Connection

Commas in a Series
■ *Proofreader's Guide* pages 406–407
■ *GrammarSnap* Commas in a Series
■ *SkillsBook* pages 15–16

Capitalization
■ *Proofreader's Guide* page 420 (+)
■ *GrammarSnap* Capitalization

Subject-Verb Agreement
■ *Write Source* pages 344–345
■ *GrammarSnap* Subject-Verb Agreement

Spelling
■ *Proofreader's Guide* pages 429–431

Expository Essay **115**

Maria's Editing

I can teach you how to grow a flower.
Y
you need a clay pot, some potting soil,
=
and a flower seed. you also need water
=
and sunlight. Then just follow these steps.

First, put some potting soil in the

clay pot. Next, make a little hole in the

dirt. Drop a flower seed into the hole.

Cover it up with dirt. Now put the pot

near a sunny window. Then give the seed

a little water every day. Soon, a tiny,

green plant will grow. Be sure it gets

sunlight and water. Finally, a pretty
bloom
flower will bloum.

Edit ▶ **Check for conventions.**

1. Check your revised essay for conventions.
2. Ask a partner to check for conventions, too.
3. Mark any errors and correct them.

Maria's Editing

Review the editing changes made to the sample draft. Ask students to explain the changes and the conventions rules that go with the call-outs.

■ The three lines under both *y*'s show that the *y* should be capitalized because *you* is the first word of each sentence. The first word of every sentence should be capitalized.

■ The circle around the period shows that end punctuation was added. Every sentence ends with a punctuation mark. Most commands end with a period.

■ The circled word shows that the writer corrected the spelling of the word.

Sometimes spelling mistakes are simply missed. Sometimes students make an effort to write a word based on what they know about letter patterns. Remind students that they can **use a dictionary** (*see below*) to check the spelling of a word.

Teaching Tip: Use a Dictionary

Students may benefit from a refresher on how to use a dictionary to check the spelling of a word. (See SE page 389.)

● Review the process for using guide words and the alphabet to find a word. Write a couple of commonly misspelled words on the board, or ask students to suggest words from their essay. Ask volunteers to

demonstrate how to find the word in a dictionary to check its spelling.

● Point out that if they have used what they know about sounds and letter patterns to attempt to spell the word, then the correctly spelled word is probably nearby, in an entry on the same page, or on the preceding or following page.

● Point out that sometimes words surprise writers because they are

not spelled the way they sound (for example, *know* and *no*). It may be difficult to find a word with a surprising spelling in the dictionary. Good writers check their spelling lists and ask a partner for help.

✳ For a list of important words second-grade writers use and a list of homophones, see SE pages 429–445.

Publishing Sharing Your Essay

Have students photocopy the final copy of their essays to share with classmates and other students who may wish to try the activity. Place the how-to essays in a booklet. Or glue each essay to a separate piece of oak tag or cardboard, laminate it, and place it in a bin with the others.

How-to essays provide the groundwork for demonstration speeches (see below).

Technology Connections

Remind students that they can use the Writing Network features of the Portfolio to share their work with peers.

* **Write Source Online** *Portfolio*
* **Write Source Online** **Net-text**

116

Publishing ▶ Sharing Your Essay
Maria's How-To Essay

How to Grow a Flower

I can teach you how to grow a flower. You need a clay pot, some potting soil, and a flower seed. You also need water and sunlight. Then just follow these steps.

First, put some potting soil in the clay pot. Next, make a little hole in the dirt. Drop a flower seed into the hole. Cover it up with dirt. Now put the pot near a sunny window. Then give the seed a little water every day. Soon, a tiny, green plant will grow. Be sure it gets sunlight and water. Finally, a pretty flower will bloom.

I like growing flowers because they are pretty. It is fun to watch them grow. When they bloom, I pick them for my mom.

Publish ▶ **Share your essay.**

Advanced Learners

If time and topics allow, have students who would like to demonstrate their activities make presentations to the class.

* For information about preparing and giving speeches, see SE pages 300–305.

Have students
* use their essay to write note cards and
* bring to class all of the supplies listed in their essay.

Reflecting on Your Writing

After you finish your how-to essay, take some time to think about it. Then fill in a sheet like this about your essay.

Thinking About Your Writing

Name: _Maria_

Title: _How to Grow a Flower_

1. The best thing about my essay is

   that I put the steps in the

   right order.

2. The main thing I learned while writing my essay is _that it is important to_

   sound confident.

Provide photocopies of the reproducible Thinking About Your Writing sheet (TE page 501) for students to use as they reflect on their writing.

Tell students not to copy the ideas shown on the sample sheet. Reflecting on their own writing experiences is meant to help them become better writers.

One way for students to figure out the best thing about their essay is to think about any favorable comments they may have received from their classmates and from you when they shared their essay.

Writer's Craft

Reflections: You've probably heard the expression "Writing is thinking on paper." When students revise and edit their writing, they deepen their thinking. When they reflect upon their writing, they can gain a new perspective on their thoughts. The long term for this process is *metacognition*—a crucial ability for students to develop as they move up through the grades.

So, by completing this simple reflection sheet, your students are starting to develop mental muscles that will help them throughout their school careers and into the workplace.

English Language Learners

Some students may need additional assistance to write their responses on the reflection sheet. Offer students individual conferences in which you discuss their strengths and what they have learned. List their responses to both questions. After the conference, give them the response list and help them choose one idea to respond to each question.

Using a Rubric

Remind students that a rubric is a chart of the traits of good writing that helps you to

- plan your writing during prewriting,
- make changes to your writing during revising, and
- judge your final copy when you finish writing (see Writing for Assessment, SE pages 124–125).

The rubrics in this book are based on a six-point scale, in which a score of 6 indicates an amazing piece of writing and a score of 1 means the writing is incomplete.

Explain to students that they will most likely have different ratings for each trait. For example, they may give themselves a 5 for ideas but a 4 for organization.

.118

Using a Rubric

The rubric on these pages can help you rate your writing.

English Language Learners

If students are using this rubric during revising and editing, they may benefit from hearing their essay read aloud by a partner, so that they can listen for places where they need to correct punctuation.

- Have students listen for statements that require periods and indicate them by placing their palms down.
- Have students listen for sentences where the voice naturally rises, indicating a question mark, and indicate them by placing their palms up.
- And have students listen for sentences with excitement, requiring an exclamation point, and indicate them by placing their palms against their chest.

Give students time to make corrections to their essay as needed.

Expository Essay   **119**

Literature Connections: You can find expository writing in *Basket Weaving* by Becky Manfredini.

Keep Trying!

3   **2**   **1**

3 More details are needed.	2 Details that don't fit the topic confuse the reader.	1 The topic is not clear.
3 Some parts are not in order.	2 All parts of the essay run together.	1 The order of information is confusing.
3 Sometimes, the voice sounds confident.	2 For the most part, the voice of the writing is unclear.	1 The writing lacks voice.
3 Errors may confuse the reader.	2 Errors make the essay hard to understand.	1 Help is needed to make corrections.

Literature Connections

Basket Weaving by Becky Manfredini tells about the Native American art of basket making. Point out that each section of this expository text explains something different about basket weaving.

Discuss how the organization of the text helps make it easier to read and understand. For additional expository models, see the Reading-Writing Connections beginning on page TE-36.

Writing
Across the Curriculum
Science: An Animal Report

Ask students if they have ever had to write a report. Invite them to share the topics about which they wrote and to tell what they learned about the topic as they wrote the report.

Explain that whenever they write a report, they are using expository writing to explain a topic.

Then read the sample report together and ask students to point out specific details that tell what the animal looks like, what it eats, and where it lives.

120

Writing
Across the Curriculum
Science: An Animal Report

In her science class, Kelli wrote an expository essay about warthogs.

Warthogs

Beginning   Warthogs look like hairy pigs. They have tusks, long legs, and warts on their faces. Sometimes, birds sit on their backs. The birds eat bugs that live on the warthog.

Middle   What do you think warthogs eat? They eat grass and seeds. They also like berries, bark, and roots. Once in a while, warthogs even eat bugs and dead animals!

Ending   Warthogs live in Africa. They like to hide in aardvark tunnels. When predators come along, warthogs charge at them with their sharp tusks. Stay away from warthogs!

Materials

Photograph of warthog (TE p. 120)

Copy Masters

Venn Diagram (TE p. 120)

Gathering Chart (TE p. 121)

English Language Learners

Familiarize students with the topic by showing them a photograph of a warthog. Read Kelli's first paragraph and use the photograph to point out the physical features she describes. Then use the reproducible Venn Diagram (TE page 512) to compare and contrast warthogs with pigs. For a model Venn diagram, see SE page 380.

Writing in Science   **121**

Writing Tips

Before You Write

Think of an animal.

Read about the animal.

Answer three questions about it.

Gathering Questions

Animal: _____

1. What does it look like?
2. What does it eat?
3. Where does it live?

During Your Writing

Name the animal and tell what it looks like in the beginning.

Explain what it eats in the middle.

Describe where it lives in the ending.

After You Have Written

Revise your writing so that every part is clear.

Check for capitalization, punctuation, and spelling errors.

Make a neat final copy.

Writing Tips

Before You Write

Encourage students to choose an animal that they are interested in learning more about and one about which their readers may know little or nothing.

Distribute photocopies of the reproducible Gathering Chart (TE page 533) for students to use to gather their information.

✳ For more help on finding information for a report, have students turn to SE pages 258–271.

During Your Writing

Encourage students to follow the order and pattern of sentences in each paragraph of the sample animal report on SE page 120.

After You Have Written

Suggest that students exchange reports with a partner. Tell partners to read the report and circle anything they don't understand.

English Language Learners

Have students use the Gathering Chart to list characteristics of an animal that they're familiar with. Encourage students to write about an animal from their native country.

Struggling Learners

Give students practice in supplying details. Write the name of a common animal, such as a rooster, on the board. Have students take turns giving details such as *crows "cock-a-doodle-doo," eats corn, lives on a farm.* Repeat with other animals. Suggest that students use this strategy when they gather details for their charts.

Advanced Learners

Explain that writers often use titles with a "twist" to capture their reader's attention. Have students work together on a list of animals for reports and create engaging titles such as
- Hairy Pigs (warthogs)
- Clocks with Feathers (roosters)
- Stretch! (giraffes)

Practical Writing: An Invitation

Help students make the connection between the expository writing they have done and writing an invitation. Help them identify the details that "explain" in the body of the invitation.

- The first sentence explains **who** is having the event (Paulo's class) and **what** the event is (a Thanksgiving play).
- The next two sentences explain **where** (Room 44) and **when** the event takes place (November 24, at two o'clock).
- The next two sentences explain more about the play itself. (Paulo will be a Pilgrim. The play will show how the Pilgrims made Thanksgiving dinner.)

You may want to discuss the parts of a friendly letter. Return to this sample letter whenever students write friendly letters throughout the year.

122

Practical Writing: An Invitation

In class, Paulo wrote an invitation. He asked his aunt to come to a special event at his school.

Date

November 4, 2011

Greeting

Dear Aunt Rosa,

Body Sentences

Our class is having a play to celebrate Thanksgiving. It will be in Room 44 on November 24. The play begins at two o'clock. I will be a Pilgrim in the play. We will show how the Pilgrims made their Thanksgiving dinner. Let me know if you can come.

Closing

Love,

Signature

Paulo

Copy Masters

5 W's Chart (TE p. 123)

Grammar Connection

Commas
- **Proofreader's Guide** pages 408–409
- **GrammarSnap** Commas in Dates and Addresses
- **SkillsBook** pages 25–26

English Language Learners

Explain to students that *closing* in writing means *ending* and that the closing of a letter is a word or phrase used to end a letter. List several closings students can use, such as *Love, Your friend, Yours truly,* and *Sincerely,* depending on the person receiving the letter. Point out that the first word of a closing begins with a capital letter.

Practical Writing   **123**

Writing Tips

5 W's Chart

Before You Write

Think of a special event.

Answer the 5 W questions about the event.

Who is holding the event?
What is the event?
When and **where** will it be?
Why should people attend?

Who?	
What?	
When?	
Where?	
Why?	

During Your Writing

Begin with the date and the greeting.
Answer the 5 W's in the body sentences.
Use a closing like **Love** or **Your friend** and sign your name.

After You Have Written

Change any parts that could be improved.
Correct any errors and make a neat copy.

Writing Tips

Before You Write

Use the sample invitation on SE page 122 to review the basic form of a friendly letter (date, greeting, body sentences, closing, and signature). Tell students to follow this form as they write their invitation.

✳ Also see SE page 408 for comma rules related to letters.

If your class or school has a future event planned, provide students with details and have students write their invitation for this event.

Distribute photocopies of the reproducible 5 W's Chart (TE page 508).

During Your Writing

Remind students to begin their body sentences by telling who is having the event. For sample wording, students can look at the sample invitation on SE page 122.

After You Have Written

Students who write an invitation to an actual upcoming event can send their invitations through regular mail, or they can use e-mail. Have them refer to SE page 154 to address their envelopes, or assist them with sending their e-mail invitations.

English Language Learners

Students may benefit from brainstorming ideas aloud as a group before they begin their 5 W's chart. To help focus the discussion on special events, have partners discuss several reasons to have a celebration. Afterward, have them use their ideas to begin their prewriting.

Writing for Assessment

If your students must take school, district, or state assessments this year, focus on the writing form on which they will be tested.

In addition to responding to a prompt, this lesson can also be an opportunity for students to practice evaluating an expository essay. Using the rubric for expository writing (SE pages 118–119) and the reproducible Assessment Sheet (TE page 499), work with students to score the sample essay on SE page 125. (A completed assessment sheet is provided on TE page 489 for your benefit.) Two additional essays are available in copy master form (see **Benchmark Papers** box below). Again, a completed assessment sheet is provided for each benchmark paper.

124

Writing for Assessment

On most writing tests, you will read a prompt and write a paragraph about it.

Writing Prompt

Think of a game you like to play. Write a paragraph that explains how to play it. Tell why you like the game.

Think   Yoshi thought about games he has played.

List   He listed some and circled the one he wanted to write about.

Draw   Then Yoshi drew a picture to help him write his paragraph.

List of Ideas

> Games I like to play
>   kickball
>   (the snail)
>   baseball

Yoshi's Drawing

Copy Masters

Assessment Sheet (TE p. 124)

Materials

Chart paper (TE p. 125)

Benchmark Papers

How to Write a Report (good)
TE pp. 490–491

Making Bracelets (poor)
TE pp. 492–493

English Language Learners

Some students may read prompts without understanding them. Have students practice reading prompts and then restating them in their own words. Point out key words and phrases in the prompt such as:

• *explains* (makes clear)
• *how to* (steps that tell how to play the game)
• *tell why* (give reasons)

Yoshi's How-To Paragraph

The topic sentence names the game.

Learn to Play Snail

I know a game called snail. First, you draw a really big snail on the sidewalk. Give the snail an open mouth and a huge stomach. Then put a small stone into the snail's mouth. Hop on one foot and try to kick the stone into the stomach and back to the mouth. If you do it, you get one point. If you touch a line, you don't get a point. Each player takes five turns. The player with the most points wins. I love this game because it is fun to hop.

The body sentences tell how to play the game.

The closing sentence gives a final idea.

practice

1. Make a list of games you play.
2. Choose your topic and draw a picture (if you wish).
3. Write your paragraph.

Point out that the assessment writing prompt asks students to do the same expository type of writing they did earlier in their directions paragraphs about *how to* go from one place to another (SE pages 90–95). This prompt asks for directions that explain *how to* play a game.

Yoshi's How-to Paragraph

Have students brainstorm a list of games that they know how to play. Then select two or three games from the list that all students know how to play and review the rules for playing each game. This will ensure that all students have a suitable topic for the **Practice** activity and that they can recall the basic rules of the game. Students can add their own comments about why they enjoy the game at the end of the paragraph to make their writing more personal and unique.

English Language Learners

Students may feel more comfortable choosing a game they learned in their first language or culture. Provide opportunities for them to teach the game to the class orally, while a volunteer lists the steps on chart paper. Then have them use the list to develop their paragraphs.

Struggling Learners

Students may want to use Yoshi's first sentence as a sentence starter. Suggest they use words from the prompt on SE page 124 to craft different beginnings such as:

- _____ is a fun game I would like to tell you about.
- Do you like to play games?
- Here is a game you can play whenever you want.

Advanced Learners

Challenge students to write the directions for a game that requires more steps than the number Yoshi used in his paragraph. Motivate students by telling them that clear, easy-to-follow steps help the reader understand the game. Then have students read their paragraphs and play the games as a class.

Persuasive Writing Overview

Common Core Standards Focus

Writing 1: Write opinion pieces in which they introduce the topic or book they are writing about, state an opinion, supply reasons that support the opinion, use linking words (e.g., because, and, also) to connect opinion and reasons, and provide a concluding statement or section.

Language 2: Demonstrate command of the conventions of standard English capitalization, punctuation, and spelling when writing.

Writing Forms

- Persuasive Paragraph
- Persuasive Letter
- Across the Curriculum
- Writing for Assessment

Focus on the Traits

- **Ideas** Expressing an opinion and supporting it with strong reasons
- **Organization** Creating a beginning with a clear opinion statement, a middle that includes reasons that support it, and an ending that asks the reader to do something
- **Voice** Using strong words that convince the reader
- **Conventions** Checking for errors in capitalization, punctuation, and spelling

 Literature Connections

- *Saving Money* by Mary Firestone
- *No Helmet? Pay Up!* (an article in Harcourt *Storytown*)

 Technology Connections

 Write Source Online
www.hmheducation.com/writesource

- Net-text
- Bookshelf
- GrammarSnap
- Portfolio
- Writing Network features
- File Cabinet

 Interactive Whiteboard Lessons

Suggested Persuasive Writing Unit (Four Weeks)

Day	Writing and Skills Instruction	Student Edition		SkillsBook	Daily Language Workouts	Write Source Online
		Persuasive Writing Unit	Resource Units*			
1–5 (WEEK 1)	**Persuasive Paragraph: A Class Need** (Model, Prewriting, Writing, Revising, Editing) — Literature Connections *Saving Money*	128–135			34–35, 94	Interactive Whiteboard Lessons
	Skills Activities:					
	• Pronouns		334, 462–463	127–128		GrammarSnap
	• Fragments		356, 449 (+)	103–104		GrammarSnap
opt.	*Giving Speeches*	304–305				
6 (WEEK 2)	**Persuasive Essay: A Persuasive Letter** (Model)	136–139			36–37, 95	
7–10	(Prewriting, Writing)	140–143				Net-text
11–13	(Revising)	144–149			38–39, 96	Net-text
	Working with a Partner	16–19				
	Skills Activities:					
	• Adjectives to compare		349, 472–473	149–150		GrammarSnap
	• Verbs		340 (+), 464 (+)	135–136		GrammarSnap
	• Nouns (possessive)		332, 460–461	125–126		GrammarSnap
14–15 (WEEK 3)	(Editing)	150–151				Net-text
	Skills Activities:					
	• Commas (in dates and addresses)		408 (+)	23–24, 45–46, 49–50, 51–52		GrammarSnap
	• Capitalization, abbreviations		402 (+), 418 (+), 426–427	5–6, 43–44, 79–80, 81, 82		GrammarSnap
	• Mechanics review		417–426 (+), 428	85–86		
	• Spelling		432–433			
16–18	(Publishing, Reflecting) — Literature Connections *No Helmet? Pay Up!*	152–157			40–41, 97	Portfolio, Net-text
opt.	*Giving Speeches*	304–305				
19–20 (WEEK 4)	**Persuasive Writing Across the Curriculum** (Science, Social Studies)	158–161				
	Persuasive Writing for Assessment	162–163				
	Skills Activity:					
	• Commas (between city and state)			21–22		GrammarSnap

* These units are also located in the back of the *Teacher's Edition*. Resource Units include "Basic Grammar and Writing," "A Writer's Resource," and "Proofreader's Guide."
(+) This activity is located in a different section of the *Write Source Student Edition*. If students have already completed this activity, you may wish to review it at this time.

Teacher's Notes for Persuasive Writing

This overview for persuasive writing includes some specific suggestions for teaching this unit.

Writing Focus

Persuasive Paragraph (pages 128–135)

In persuasive writing, the writer expresses an opinion, gives reasons for having the opinion, and tries to persuade others to agree. This chapter explains each step students need to take in order to write a convincing persuasive paragraph. The model features the argument for getting 10 hours of sleep each night.

Persuasive Letter (pages 136–157)

The friendly letter may not be a new writing form for your students; however, writing a persuasive letter may be new to many. A letter that seeks to persuade prepares students for real-world writing forms such as business letters that seek information (letters of request) or that call for certain actions (editorials).

The friendly letter follows a certain format. Writing this type of letter is a step-by-step process. This type of letter also calls for a persuasive voice that is both serious and convincing. Part of sounding convincing depends on having solid reasons and support for an opinion.

Across the Curriculum (pages 158–161)

Persuasive writing in other disciplines may not be as common as descriptive, narrative, or expository writing. In this chapter, a student in science class writes a paragraph to promote saving tigers. In social studies, a student creates a flier to promote (another persuasive purpose for writing) an upcoming class event.

Writing for Assessment (pages 162–163)

In this open-ended prompt, the student shares an opinion about a possible class trip and gives three solid reasons why it would be a good destination. Students may be more adept at supporting their opinions than they realize. Encourage them to think of all the times they have tried to persuade parents, family, or friends to agree with them about what to eat, where to go, what to do, and so on.

Academic Vocabulary

Read aloud the academic terms, as well as the descriptions and questions. Model for students how to read one question and answer it. Have partners monitor their understanding and seek clarification of the terms by working through the meanings and questions together.

126

Persuasive Writing

WRITE SOURCE Online

Writing Focus
- Persuasive Paragraph
- Persuasive Letter
- Across the Curriculum
- Writing for Assessment

Academic Vocabulary

Work with a partner. Read the meanings and share answers to the questions.

1. When you persuade someone, you get him or her to believe or act a certain way.
   When might you persuade someone?
2. An opinion is how you feel about something.
   What is your opinion about today's weather?
3. If a fact supports a statement, it helps show that the statement is true.
   What facts might support this statement: We need to save water?

Minilessons

Why? Why? Why? — Persuasive Paragraph

- **INVITE** students to express an opinion about a favorite place to a partner. Then have the partner **ASK**, "Why is that your favorite place?" The partner should **ASK**, "Why is that your favorite place?" three times. Each time **HAVE** the student respond with a good reason for why this place is one of her or his favorite places.

Hear, Ye! Hear, Ye! — Persuasive Letter

- **ASK** students to **CHOOSE** a nonfiction book that they enjoyed reading. (There may be as many books as students.)
  - **HAVE** them each **WRITE** a persuasive letter to the class that will inspire others to read the book.

127

Healthy kids are happy kids! That is one child's **opinion,** or personal feeling. When you state an opinion, you let others know how you feel about a topic.

In persuasive writing, you try to get the reader to accept your opinion. If you are really persuasive, you may even be able to convince the reader to take action!

Literature Connections: You can find persuasive language in *Saving Money* by Mary Firestone.

Family Connection Letters

As you begin this unit, send home the Persuasive Writing Family Connection letter, which describes what students will be learning.

● Letter in English (TE p. 566)
● Letter in Spanish (TE p. 574)

Persuasive Writing

Talk about the words *opinion* and *persuasive*. Challenge students to explain what each word means—or work with students to find the definitions in a dictionary. Help students understand the following:

■ An *opinion* is what someone thinks about a topic.
■ *Persuasive* is the adjective form of the verb *persuade*, which means "to convince someone of something."

Explain that **persuasive writing** expresses a writer's *opinion* in order to *persuade* readers to share that opinion and, often, to take action.

Ask students to tell about instances in which they've tried to persuade people to agree with them about something. Responses might include trying to convince

■ a parent or guardian to let them sleep over at a friend's house,
■ siblings to agree to watch a certain television show, or
■ friends to play a game.

How successful were they at being persuasive? Can they think of a time when they just couldn't convince the other person? Tell students that this section will help them not only to write more persuasively but also to speak more persuasively.

Literature Connections

Saving Money by Mary Firestone explains why and how people save money. Like many other informational texts, this one also includes persuasive language.

Discuss the last paragraph with students. What is the author's opinion? Which words does she use to persuade young people to save money? For additional models of persuasive text, see the Reading-Writing Connections beginning on page TE-36.

Writing a
Persuasive Paragraph

Objectives

- demonstrate an understanding of the content and structure of a persuasive paragraph
- choose a topic (a way to be healthier) to write about
- plan, draft, revise, and edit a persuasive paragraph

Remind students that a paragraph is a group of sentences about a specific topic. In a **persuasive paragraph**, the topic is something the writer has an opinion about. The writer gives two or three reasons why readers should agree with that opinion and then tells readers what they should do.

✱ For more about writing paragraphs, see SE pages 364–369.

Talk with the class about familiar health and safety issues. Share materials such as public service ads and online information. Useful Internet sites include the following:

- kidshealth.org
- bam.gov (the Centers for Disease Control and Prevention page for kids)
- mypyramid.gov/kids (food pyramid information for kids)

Technology Connections

Use this unit's Interactive Whiteboard Lesson to introduce persuasive writing.

Interactive Whiteboard Lessons

128

Writing a
Persuasive Paragraph

Eva's class was discussing healthy living. She noticed how tired her friend Polly looked. It gave her an idea for a persuasive paragraph. Eva decided to write a paragraph to persuade her classmates to get more sleep.

In this chapter, you will write a paragraph to persuade your classmates to make a healthy choice.

Materials

Printed or online information about health and safety topics for kids (TE p. 128)

Dictionary (TE p. 135)

Copy Masters

Cluster (TE p. 130)

Table Diagram (TE p. 132)

Revising Checklist (TE p. 134)

Editing Checklist (TE p. 135)

Eva's Persuasive Paragraph

Go to Sleep!

Topic Sentence

You should get ten hours of sleep each night. **Sleep helps you**

Body Sentences

stay healthy and happy. It gives your body and brain a rest from a hard day. Best of all, sleep gives you energy to do fun things, like jumping rope and riding bikes. So every night,

Closing Sentence

you should get plenty of sleep!

- The topic sentence states your opinion.
- The body sentences give two or three reasons for your opinion.
- The closing sentence tells the reader what action to take.

Eva's Persuasive Paragraph

After students have read the model paragraph and reviewed each of its parts, encourage their responses by asking the following questions:

- What is Eva's opinion? (You should get ten hours of sleep.)
- How many reasons does she give for her opinion? (three)
- Which reason does Eva think is the most important? (Sleep gives you energy to do fun things.) How can you tell? (The words *Best of all* indicate that this is the most important reason.)
- What action does Eva ask readers to take? (Get plenty of sleep.)
- Do you find Eva's paragraph convincing? (Encourage students to think about their own experiences with sleep when they answer and to explain why they do or do not agree with Eva's opinion.)

English Language Learners

Students may find it difficult to identify words that signal a writer's opinion. Direct their attention to the topic sentence, and point out that *should* is a word that writers often use to express an opinion. Explain that some people may think you should get ten hours of sleep each night, but others might not agree.

Before students write an opinion (topic) sentence (SE page 131), provide oral practice in stating clear opinions. Ask students to complete sentence starters such as the following:

- The best kind of pet to own is . . .
- I should learn how to . . .
- Our class needs . . .

Prewriting Choosing Your Topic

Provide photocopies of the reproducible Cluster (TE page 504) for students to use as they think of topics. Encourage them to think of at least two possibilities, and explain that it's okay to leave circles on the cluster blank. If students come up with more ideas than there are circles, tell them to add more circles.

✳ For more about making a cluster, see SE page 381.

Explain that writing about something they are interested in will usually help students to write well. To help them feel more engaged, encourage students to choose a topic that interests them and to which they feel a connection. For example:

- Topic—Get lots of exercise.
  Connection—After I joined a soccer team, I had more energy.
- Topic—Brush your teeth twice a day.
  Connection—Our new electric toothbrush almost made brushing my teeth fun. The next time I went to the dentist, I didn't have any cavities.

130

Prewriting ▶ Choosing Your Topic

To plan a persuasive paragraph, you first must select a strong topic.

This is what Eva did to find a topic for her paragraph. Eva thought about her class discussion. She then made a cluster of topic ideas and starred the strongest topic.

Topic Cluster

Prewrite ▶ **Choose your topic.**

1. Think about what you have learned about healthy living.
2. Make a cluster of topic ideas. Star the one you want to write about.

English Language Learners

Work with students to complete the "healthy living" cluster. Then discuss how each choice can make them healthier. Based on their discussions, have students select the idea they think they can best support with good reasons. Point out that choosing the idea they know most about can make writing a strong persuasive paragraph easier.

Advanced Learners

Have students work as a group to brainstorm as many topics as possible that relate to healthy choices. Assist students by suggesting that they narrow the categories shown in Eva's cluster. For example, "eat fruit and vegetables as often as possible" is more specific than "eat healthy foods."